INDIAN CHUTNEYS, RAITAS, PICKLES & PRESERVES

A complete range of accompaniments using a wealth of natural foods to
provide delicious vegetarian side dishes which will suit every taste
and every occasion.

J. S. REEH.
Nov. 1987

By the same author
INDIAN VEGETARIAN COOKING

Indian CHUTNEYS RAITAS, PICKLES & PRESERVES

by

Michael Pandya

Illustrated by Paul Turner

THORSONS PUBLISHING GROUP
Wellingborough · New York

Published in the UK by Thorsons Publishing Group
Denington Estate, Wellingborough, Northamptonshire NN8 2RQ
and in the USA by Thorsons Publishers Inc., 377 Park Avenue South,
New York, NY 10016. Thorsons Publishers Inc. are distributed to the
trade by Inner Traditions International Ltd, New York.

First published 1986

© MICHAEL PANDYA 1986

*All rights reserved. No part of this book may be reproduced or utilized in any form or by any
means, electronic or mechanical, including photocopying, recording or by any information
storage and retrieval system, without permission in writing from the Publisher.*

British Library Cataloguing in Publication Data

Pandya, Michael
    Indian chutneys, raitas, pickles and preserves.
    1. Vegetarian cookery   2. Cookery, Indian
    I. Title

ISBN 0-7225-1167-1

Printed and Bound in Great Britain by
Whitstable Litho Ltd., Whitstable, Kent

DEDICATION
To all the Pandyas from Lal Phatak, Kanpur —
wherever in the world they may be living today!

Contents

Acknowledgements

My kitchen deity and dearest mother — Amma as I called her — was responsible for my initiation into the magnificence of Indian food at an early age. My interest in the kitchen and the cookery concoctions developed from there. My revered father — Babuji — taught me other things, like how I must concentrate on whatever I choose to do, and must try to do it well. How pleased Amma and Babuji would be to see what I have been able to do, and to note therefrom that their teachings have not been totally in vain! I hope my parents' blessings will always show me the way.

Last year I paid a "flying" visit to India to see how the pickling traditions have matured there over the years. I remember that as a child I used to watch every summer (when schools were closed and all the relatives were paying us a visit) my mother and other older ladies of Lal Phatak — my family home in Kanpur, India, — making, or supervising the making of, sweet and sour pickles, preserves, and many other dishes of the ilk which can be made in advance; the family children were at times allowed to help. As the day progressed, out came the bottles, crocks, and jars, and the preparations would mature in the baking sun while the family stayed indoors under the fan. Before it was time for the schools to reopen after the summer recess, and the relatives to disperse, the whole Pandya clan would have plenty of supplies to last them until the next summer.

My mausi and mausa (my mother's sister and her husband) were the wizards of pickles and preserves. My mausa's family owned a whole village near Allahabad and all kinds of vegetables and fruits were available to them in large quantities for pickles and preserves. Mausi and mausa used to lead a rather large team of men and women in the annual pickle-making gala in their village, keenly witnessed and admired by many novices and outsiders. At the end of the season, they had enough pickles and preserves for several families for several months. Suddenly last year my mausi and mausa were no more, but the village tradition has been kept going by the next generation.

The young population of India today seems generally to have become somewhat lazy; also, everyone seems to have less time. If, therefore, you occasionally detect an odd couple or two smuggling into their homes a ready-made jar of pickles or preserves from the stores, you have to forgive them. By and large, though, there must still be literally tons of pickles and preserves made in Indian homes throughout the summer months every year.

My two sisters — Jiya at Bareilly, and Munni at Mawana — have kept the Pandya family's traditions going in their husbands' homes, and their daughters are picking up the secrets fast! As always, I discussed this book with my sisters and picked their brains on the subject generally, collecting some ingredients and props in the process. Jiya's daughter, Rashmi, came up with some useful suggestions for the book, which I readily accepted; thank you Rashmi. No cookbook of mine can be complete without my tributes to the culinary talents of my Chhoti mami, whom I went to see at Lucknow. The plan and details of this book came up for discussion and her advice was sought and obtained.

Introduction

They say variety is the spice of life. You will find plenty of variety in this book — and no dearth of spices either! In addition, the dishes covered in this book easily lend themselves to further experimentation and variety. Although it is true to say that Indian cookery *per se* does not need any introduction in the West, the groups of dishes included in this work are not all that well known here. It is yet to be discovered in the West, for instance, that most Indian chutneys, pickles, and raitas can be made very quickly. I have realized that only too often during my trips up and down the country, doing demonstrations or making items for television, or while doing a filming or photo session at home where non-Indians of an uninitiated variety are involved. I do hope that this book will help remove that lacuna from the western learning about Indian cuisine.

This book contains separate sections on chutneys, sauces, raitas, salads and kachumbers, pickles, and preserves. These preparations have been made in India since time immemorial. Most of them are made from fresh seasonal and other standard vegetables, herbs, and fruits. India is a veritable paradise for these items, which are grown almost without number in most parts of that country. Visitors to India have been amazed by the abundance and cheapness as well as by the enormous number of fruits and vegetables available there. The glorious year-round sunshine and the climate of India are particularly suited to the dishes which have to be baked or matured in the sun, e.g. the pickles.

Chutneys are the most popular dishes, made from fresh vegetables, fruits, and herbs. They can be put together quickly, often at the last minute, by chopping and/or grinding together a few ingredients and adding water or lemon juice. Chutneys and kachumbers are palate teasers; they supply a sharp contrast in taste to simple and bland meals. They also provide the much needed protein and vitamins, and tingle the brain. These dishes add colour to the meal and should be selected carefully and with imagination to complement the rest of the meal. Chutneys should be made freshly for each meal wherever possible, and should not be kept for days; they usually improve when served chilled. Sauces like chutneys inject a peculiar and intriguing flavour into food and add the crowning touch, turning an ordinary dull dish into a tasty and colourful superstar!

Yogurt has for ages been one of the most versatile ingredients of Indian cuisine, and one that has earned international recognition as an excellent health food. The best-known Indian yogurt dish is the raita. Raitas are interesting side dishes made with a felicitous combination of plain yogurt with herbs, vegetables, and fruits; they provide a cooling contrast to an otherwise hot and spicy meal. A yogurt diet is a source of good health and longevity — such diets are still common among Indian village folk. A regular yogurt diet is believed to give people a comely and curvacious body. Lord Krishna of India spent most of his life on yogurt and other milk products, and look what he achieved — 16,000 wives (at the same time) and a host of other female companions besides!

Salad is a flexible dish that can be prepared according to desire and availability of the ingredients. It can be served as a main or side dish and, on occasion, even as a dessert! A salad can be anything from a simple bowl of crisp greens to a colourful medley of fruits and vegetables, blended with a creamy sauce and shimmering on a bed of lettuce. The key to a successful salad is that its greens should be crisp when served, and that it should be served chilled. A salad must also have eye appeal as well as please the palate.

Pickles enjoy a high position in the Indian culinary calendar. Every year mothers and grannies in villages prepare their annual quota of pickles, preserves, and other family specialities which can be made in advance and last for the most part of the year. During the summer months they use the whole family in trimming, peeling, and cutting the vegetables and fruits. Using their tremendous expertise, and with alacrity and enthusiasm, they make these dishes for the next twelve months, knowing they will please their children and grandchildren, relatives, neighbours and friends. Given that people have limited time to spare in this day and age, I have concentrated on those pickles and preserves which can be made relatively quickly and easily, and last for a while. Pickles sharpen the appetite and give the lethargic system a fresh charge; among them they offer a taste for every tongue!

India is the home of many fragrant spices. Spices are used in one form or another in most recipes in this book, and lead to superb tastes and preparations. The key to success in Indian cooking lies not in heaping spices over the dishes, nor in making them acrid or searing, but rather in the delicacy of spicing which creates flavours and tastes irrespective of whether the dish is hot or bland. It was indeed the lure of spices which first brought the Europeans to Indian shores. These spices, once the pride and joy of India, later became the cause of its subjugation at the hands of the British!

India's zest for life is amply demonstrated in its culinary dexterity and in its variety in all types of food. An old Indian proverb pronounces that the making and eating of food are divine gifts and should therefore be received with joy and respect. In consequence Indian kitchens are treated as something like temples, and there is an outpouring of divine dishes from them all the time. A home-cooked Indian meal is an event and can be most exciting. You get plenty of choice, and all the chutneys, pickles, and raitas to tickle your taste buds. Differences in climate and local produce add a lot to variety. By tradition, Indian cooking techniques and the specialities of each family are handed down by word of mouth or demonstration from mother or father to daughter or son; written cookery books are a modern phenomenon. Good male cooks in India are a valuable treasure, recognized by all levels of society. In the Mughal era distinguished male chefs were appointed to the royal court!

Whether male or female, read the book and get ready to delight your family and friends.

Start by using the subtle aromatic spices and the natural aroma of vegetables and fruits to tempt your guests to the dining table; then let them feast their eyes on the *mélange* of colour and texture, alternating from the cooling whites of the raita, through other main dishes and glowing reds of sauces and pickles, to the luscious green of the chutneys. End the meal with delicious preserves which have a reputation for curing the heart (but, alas, not broken hearts) and sharpening the brain. Leave your guests breathless in admiration for your panache and prowess in the art of making the Indian relishes, raitas, pickles, and preserves.

Bon appetit!

Batterie de Cuisine

(Chauke ke Khaas Bartan)

It helps to create an Indian atmosphere in and around your kitchen, especially when making Indian dishes. Psychologically, it should add to your confidence and give you a homely feeling if you start with typical Indian utensils and tools. Given below are some Indian tools, implements, and utensils used in creating the dishes in this book. Most of them are available from your Indian grocer, so get cooking!

BHAGONA — a heavy saucepan made of various metals such as stainless steel. "Batloi" and "degchi" are slightly different versions of "bhagona", or deep cooking pots.

CHAMCHA — a large spoon made of metal or wood and used for serving many foods, such as pickles, preserves, and raitas.

CHHALNI — a wooden or metal sieve, fine or otherwise, for straining liquids and ground ingredients.

JHANNA — a spoon with a long handle and a perforated disc at the end, used for making many savouries and draining food from a deep fryer or "kadhai".

KADDUKAS — a traditional Indian grater, made of metal and standing on four feet; normally used for grating fruits, vegetables, and nuts.

KADHAI — a wide-mouthed, deep or shallow metal pan with round handles on both sides, resembling a Chinese wok; normally used for deep-frying.

KARCHHI — a wooden or metallic stirrer used for frying, turning over, and stirring; long-handled spoon with a flat disc at the end of it.

KHALLA-MUSARIA — also known as IMAAMDUSTA, it is a cast-iron cousin of the mortar and pestle used for pounding hard ingredients.

SIL-BATTA — a traditional Indian grinder of herbs and spices. It consists of a pair of treated stones — a large stone slab with a rough surface known as "sil"; ingredients are placed on it and are then pressed and ground by a small round stone with a treated rough surface and known as "batta".

TARAAZU — kitchen scales for weighing ingredients.

TAWA — a griddle, usually made of cast-iron and with or without a handle, generally used for dry-roasting ingredients, especially spices, and making Indian breads.

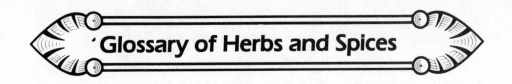

Glossary of Herbs and Spices

(Masaale Aadi ka Shabdakosh)

Flavour makes Indian food; aromatic herbs and spices are added to the various Indian dishes to enhance their tantalizing value, without reducing their nutrients or affecting their natural taste. Most spices and herbs promote appetite and are good for health, but they should be used in moderation.

Most spices are available in "whole" form so they can be ground fresh whenever possible; they begin to lose their flavour if kept for long periods of time. Keep the spices in a cool, dark, and dry place, storing them in airtight containers.

The secret of all the ingredients listed below lies in knowing when to use them and in what form, as well as their proportions and combinations.

ANISEED (ANISE SEED) (Patlee Saunf): A seed of the anise plant used in cordials, pickles, and sweets; also served after a meal. It is said to prevent flatulence.

ASAFOETIDA (Heeng): Often used in pickles and other vegetarian preparations; a strong digestive gum resin, usually available only in powdered form in the West.

BLACK PEPPERCORNS (Gol Mirchen): The first spice discovered by man and rich in vitamin C, cures fevers and heart problems. They are berries from the pepper vine, dried and hardened by the sun into black and brittle seeds and used ground or whole.

CAPSICUM (GREEN PEPPER) (Simla Mirch): Rich in vitamin C, this is a fleshy variety of green chilli that is very mild in taste; used in pickles, chutneys, and salads and many other things besides.

CARDAMOM (Illaichi): This is of two types, "brown" (bari), used in ground spices and pickles; or "green" (chhoti), white or greenish little pods containing fragrant and digestive seeds. Used in sweet dishes and preserves and some sweet pickles.

CAROM SEEDS (Ajwain): Also known as thymol seeds, and for its cough curing propensities, a digestive and carminative spice frequently used in sour pickles.

CAYENNE (Pisee Laal Mirch): Ground hottest red chillies; use sparingly until you know your capacity.

CHILLIES (Mirchen): These are of two varieties, "green" (hari), which are normally more pungent than red ones and add flavour to chutneys and food generally, or "red" (laal), which can be used whole or ground. Use with care, or your stomach will feel a burning sensation.

CINNAMON (Dall Cheeni): Used as sticks or in powdered form for flavouring pickles and other sweet and savoury preparations; a germicidal spice.

CLOVES (Laung): These are dried-up flower buds, used in sweet and savoury pickles and spice powders; a strong antiseptic agent.

CORIANDER (CILANTRO) (Dhania): It is used in two forms, as seeds — either whole, crushed, or ground, or as fresh green leaves. Coriander seeds are used in different forms in all types of pickles and chutneys and are a powerful carminative. Green coriander (a look-alike without the aroma is parsley) is an aromatic herb and is used in chutneys, garnishes, and flavourings.

CUMIN SEEDS (Zeera): A digestive spice in seed form obtained from a plant of the caraway family. These seeds are used whole or powdered in chutneys, pickles, and other curries and savouries for preservation or flavouring; they can be white or black.

FENNEL (Moti Saunf): A seed of the anise family; a rather milder and plumper variety of aniseed. Used in pickles and for flavouring; also served roasted as a post-prandial refresher.

FENUGREEK SEEDS (Methi Daane): Rich in iron, these seeds are used in pickles and spice mixtures; use them sparingly or the preparation will taste too bitter. The green leaves of the fenugreek plant are cooked as a side dish with full meals.

FRESH GINGER ROOT (Taazi Adrak): This beige-coloured root gives a pungent "kick" to the chutneys, pickles, and other dishes to which it is added in grated, chopped, or minced form. It is a carminative and has medicinal attributes.

LOTUS PUFFS (Makhaane): These are lotus seeds. When dry roasted they puff up and are used in raitas, salads, and many other delicious dishes.

MINT LEAVES (Hara Podina): An aromatic herb that can be grown in your garden; used in chutneys and raitas, and also for garnishes and flavouring.

MUSTARD SEEDS (Raai Daane): These are tiny yellow — and also black — seeds, highly nutritious and pungent; used in pickles and other dishes as a souring agent. Rich in vitamin D and manganese, they are used whole, crushed, or powdered.

NIGELLA (Kalaunji): These are little black seeds also known as onion seeds. They impart a sophisticated flavour to pickles and other vegetarian dishes in which they are used whole or roasted and ground.

SAFFRON (Kesar): The king of spices — and obviously thus expensive — is used for flavouring and colouring preserves and other sweet and savoury dishes. Saffron strands are the dried stigmata of a saffron crocus; Kashmir boasts of the most extensive crocus farming in India.

TAMARIND (Imli): A seed pod which grows on trees, used in its green or ripe form for making chutneys and sauces; it adds piquancy to yogurt dishes. Ripe tamarind (or tamarind pulp, seeded) is available in Indian grocery shops. It is first soaked in cold or warm water for varying periods of time as specified in the recipes, and then has its juice extracted; the husk is then discarded.

TURMERIC (Haldi): A distinctive yellow root spice which is usually available in the West only in powdered form; often serves as a cheaper substitute for saffron for colouring. It has a pungent flavour and is used in many pickles and other side dishes. It has digestive attributes and is often prescribed as a skin cure.

Chapter 1

Some Magical Ingredients
(Kuchh Jaadu Waali Cheezen)

Indian chefs have, over the centuries, developed some remarkable ingredients, which, when mixed in different ways with other better known ingredients, produce the exotic and remarkable tastes usually connected with Indian food. It is these magical ingredients that have raised the Indian art of cookery to the highest position in the world's food-league table, and have given Indian cuisine its uniquely enviable position. The preparation of some of these ingredients, as with the techniques of cooking and making some dishes, is even now not well known beyond the shores of India.

Some of these ingredients, which eventually lead to tantalizing tastes and fantastic flavours even within the rather narrower scope of this book, are listed below.

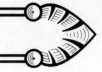

INDIAN YOGURT

(Ghar ka Dahi)

Makes   about 1¾ pints (1 litre)/4½ cups
Preparation time   10 minutes plus setting time
Cooking time   15 minutes

If heavy creamy milk (or half and half) is used, cooking time is saved in that only one boil may be adequate; ordinary milk must be boiled at least four times. What you then get is the many-splendoured ingredient of Indian cuisine. It is used in all raita dishes, and in many salads and other dishes as well as in making cold drinks.

Imperial (Metric)	American
1¾ pints (1 litre) buffalo or Jersey milk	4½ cups creamy milk (half and half)
2 fl oz (60ml) natural yogurt	⅓ cup plain yogurt

1

Boil the milk as indicated in the preceding introduction. Remove the pan, and let the milk cool for a few minutes; it should still be warm.

2

Beat the yogurt and then stir it into the milk. (Do not add yogurt when the milk is too hot or the "dahi" will not set properly. And remember — the colder the weather, the warmer the milk should be when you add yogurt.)

3

Find another container similar to the one holding milk, and pour the milk from one container to the other in quick succession. After a few times, transfer the milk to a bowl; wrap the bowl with a warm cloth and leave it in the warmest place in the house overnight.

4

In warm weather, if the bowl is placed in a cupboard, the yogurt will take no more than 5 hours to set; in a normal, centrally heated house the setting process takes about 10 to 12 hours; otherwise the yogurt can take up to 24 hours, or more, to set.

5

When set, serve the "dahi" as desired.

CREAM CHEESE

(Chhena aur Paneer)

Makes	*about 6 oz (170g/⅔ cup)*
Preparation time	*10 to 15 minutes plus setting time*
Cooking time	*10 to 15 minutes*

If using heavy buffalo or creamy milk (or half and half), only one boil may be necessary for this dish; ordinary milk must be boiled three or four times. This dish is made in two stages. At the end of the first you get "chhena", which is used mainly in sweets and in some savouries. Ultimately you have "paneer", which is used in many savouries and snacks. Both stages or varieties of this dish are used in salads.

Imperial (Metric)	American
1½ pints (900ml) milk	3¾ cups milk
1 fl oz (30ml) lemon juice	3 tablespoons lemon juice

1

Boil the milk in an ordinary saucepan; remove from the heat and let cool a little. Add the lemon juice gradually; keep stirring until the milk curdles.

2

Pour the curdled milk through a fine sieve, and gently squeeze out the whey; the remainder in the sieve is known as "chhena", it should weigh around 6 oz (170g). Use as "chhena" at this stage, according to the recipe.

3

In order to have "paneer" mould the chhena into a block and flatten it under a heavy wooden board; leave it like this about 2 hours. By then it will have set.

4

Cut into shapes, such as diamonds or squares, and use as prescribed in the particular recipes you are following.

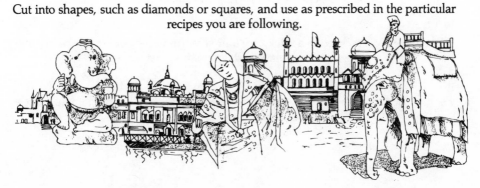

KHOYA

Cooked Milk Concentrate

Makes   about 4 oz (100g/½ cup)
Preparation time   5 minutes
Cooking time   40 minutes

Khoya is also known as *khoa* and *mawa*; it is used in making many Indian desserts and sweetmeats. *Khoya* can be either plain or granulated; the recipe given here is for the latter variety, which is used to make stunning confections and also some curries. To make plain *khoya*, omit the lemon juice.

Imperial (Metric)	*American*
1 pint (600ml) creamy milk	2½ cupsful creamy milk
1 teaspoon lemon juice	1 teaspoon lemon juice

1
Try to obtain buffalo or Jersey milk, or the net result will weigh less.

2
Place the milk in a heavy-based (and if possible, non-stick) saucepan and bring to the boil over a high heat.

3
Stir in the lemon juice so that the milk curdles. Reduce the heat to simmering point and continue cooking.

4
Keep stirring so that the milk does not stick to the base of the pan; as the milk thickens, stir even more vigorously. Use of a non-stick pan will save you some work, although occasional stirring will still be required.

5
When the milk is reduced to a thick, dry lump the consistency of creamy pastry and stops sizzling, your stylish granular *khoya* is ready.

6
Remove the pan from the heat, transfer the *khoya* into a bowl, mould it into a circle and let it cool; use as required.

Note: Left-over khoya can be stored in the refrigerator for a few days.

CLARIFIED BUTTER

(Ghee)

Makes   about 1 lb (450g/2½ cups)
Preparation time   5 minutes plus cooling time
Cooking time   30 minutes

Ghee is the main medium of frying and cooking in India; use homemade for a sense of achievement and to ensure quality at the same time. A cheaper variety of ghee can also be made from some vegetable fats. Ghee can be heated to high temperatures and ensures crisp results; in some homes ghee is alternated with mustard oil.

Imperial (Metric)	American
1¼ lb (575g) plain butter	2½ cups plain butter

1

Place the butter in a heavy-based saucepan; put it over moderate heat and bring to a boil; keep stirring.

2

Lower the heat and let simmer another 20 minutes. Using a wooden spatula, remove the scum from the top from time to time.

3

Remove the pan from the heat and let cool 1 hour or so. Strain and transfer the contents into a covered container, discarding the salty residue at the bottom of the pan, and let the ghee set as it cools completely.

4

Take out the ghee, melt, and use when needed.

GARAM MASALA

(Garam Masala)

Lasts	2 months or more
Preparation time	10 minutes
Cooking time	5 minutes

"Garam masala" is a mixture of several spices ground together and, because the Hindi name for this preparation is very well known, the term has been used as such throughout the book. Strangely, every chef has his or her own recipe for this preparation; here is one of mine. Garam masala adds life to the dishes it is used in; it is essential, however, that it should stay fresh and should not be allowed to lose its flavour, so store carefully in an airtight container.

Imperial (Metric)	American
2 tablespoons coriander seeds	2 tablespoons coriander seeds
4 medium bay leaves	4 medium bay leaves
½ teaspoon each of cloves and black peppercorns	½ teaspoon each of cloves and black peppercorns
2 teaspoons each of cumin and brown cardamom seeds	2 teaspoons each of cumin and brown cardamom seeds
1 teaspoon cinnamon powder	1 teaspoon cinnamon powder

1

Heat a frying pan to a high temperature. Lower the heat to moderate, add all the ingredients, and dry roast, stirring constantly, for 2 to 3 minutes, or until the spices give off a strong, aromatic smell.

2

Remove from the heat and finely grind all the ingredients together, by hand or in an electric grinder. Push the powder through a muslin cloth (or a very fine sieve). Let the mixture cool.

3

Store in a dry, airtight container, and use as needed. Cover the container tightly after each use.

NOTE: Some people prefer to make garam masala by grinding the above ingredients without dry roasting them first; it still adds life to the dishes it is used in! See if you like it that way.

SAAMBHAR POWDER

(Saambhar Masala)

Makes about 10 oz (275g/2½ cups)
Preparation time 10 minutes
Cooking time 5 minutes

This spice powder is used mainly in making saambhar sauce; it is also used in the preparation of some other South Indian dishes. It can be made and stored in advance, and can last for several weeks. It is advisable not to make too much of it; store the powder in an airtight bag or container.

Imperial (Metric)	*American*
2 oz (50g) each of toor and urad daals	¼ cup each of toor and urad daals
1 oz (25g) each of white cumin, mustard, coriander, and fenugreek seeds	¼ cup each of white cumin, mustard, coriander, and fenugreek seeds
2 tablespoons turmeric powder	2 tablespoons turmeric powder
1 tablespoon each of dried red chillies and curry leaves	1 tablespoon each of dried red chilies and curry leaves
2 teaspoons each of black peppercorns, brown cardamom, and carom seeds	2 teaspoons each of black peppercorns, brown cardamom, and carom seeds
½ teaspoon asafoetida powder	½ teaspoon asafoetida powder

1

Heat a heavy-bottomed frying pan or kadhai of an adequate size. Dry-roast all the above ingredients, stirring constantly, over moderate heat for about 5 minutes, or until the spices give off a strong aromatic smell.

2

Remove from the heat, and grind the spices together into a powder. Push the powder through a muslin cloth and then let cool completely.

3

Store in an airtight bag or container, and keep in a dark, cool, and dry place. Serve when needed, and do not leave the powder in the open for too long.

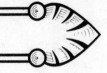

CRISPY CROÛTONS

(Kurkure Roti Tukre)

Serves	*10 helpings or more*
Preparation time	*10 minutes*
Cooking time	*10 minutes*

Croûtons add a stylish and decorative touch to such dishes as salads or soups that they are served with. Made by cubing and deep-fying bread slices, croûtons can be cooked in advance and stored in an airtight container or bag for a few days.

Imperial (Metric)	American
4 thick wholemeal slices of bread	4 thick whole wheat slices of bread
Ghee as necessary for deep-frying	Ghee as necessary for deep-frying

1
Remove the crusts, and cut the bread slices into small cubes.

2
Heat enough ghee in a kadhai or a deep frying pan, and fry the bread cubes over low heat until golden all over.

3
When cooked, remove and place on paper towels. Let cool, When cool and fully dry, store in a suitable container.

4
Serve when needed, and do not leave them in the open for too long.

SUGAR SAUCE

(Chaashni)

Makes   about 2 pints (1.2 litres/5 cups)
Preparation time   5 minutes
Cooking time   20 minutes

You can make sugar sauce, also called syrup, for preparing preserves and other sweet dishes. Although you may make this sauce in advance, it is not advisable to make too much; it sets and solidifies and has to be melted each time it is used, and thus gains in strength. This sauce can be made into many strengths by the length of time it is cooked. Either one-string or two-string consistency is sufficient for most sweet dishes.

Imperial (Metric)	*American*
3 lb (1.5kg) raw cane sugar	6 cups raw sugar
1½ pints (900ml) water	3¾ cups water

1

Place the sugar and water in a saucepan; put over high heat and bring to a boil.

2

Lower heat and go on cooking. Using a wooden spatula, remove the scum from time to time and discard it.

3

After a total of three boils the syrup should assume a one-string consistency, meaning that when a drop of syrup is pressed between your thumb and forefinger, it lifts up in one string. This takes about 1 minute.

4

Further cooking will give you two-, three-, or four-string consistencies until eventually the syrup will crack into chips known as "misree", or Indian sugar candy.

NOTE: There are several schools of thought about the proportion of sugar and water when making syrup: double the water to sugar (i.e. 1 pint water (600ml/2½ cups) to ½ lb (225g/1 cup) sugar; both on a par (1 pint (600ml/2½ cups) water to 1 lb (450g/2 cups) sugar); and half the water (½ pint (300ml/1¼ cups) water to 1 lb (450g/2 cups) sugar), as in this recipe. They are all a matter of personal taste and the dish being made. I have used other proportions in my other books; this proportion is another popular choice.

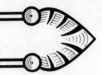

BATTER DROPS

(Boondi)

Serves 6	
Preparation time 6 minutes plus standing time	
Cooking time 10 minutes	

"Boondi" can be cooked in advance and stored in an airtight bag or container for several weeks; it is advisable not to keep them for too long. Batter drops are available in packets at Indian grocers. Watch out for the expiry date, though! "Boondi" is splendidly versatile, and many sweet and savoury dishes are made from it. Raita is one category of dish in which "boondi" will make an appearance in this book.

Imperial (Metric)	*American*
4 oz (100g) gram flour (besan)	1 cup gram flour (besan)
¼ pint (150ml) water	⅔ cups water
Ghee as necessary, for deep-frying	Ghee as necessary, for deep-frying

1

Place the gram flour in a deep bowl or another suitable container; gradually add the water and whisk into a batter, making sure that lumps do not form.

2

Add more water as needed until the batter is of a "drop" consistency. Let stand about 20 minutes.

3

Heat enough ghee in a kadhai, and leave over moderate heat. Using a jhanna (a long-handled spoon with a perforated disc), pour the batter into the hot ghee; jerk and shake the spoon, and batter drops will fall into the kadhai. With a clean spoon, turn the drops over in the ghee until they are golden all over. If your kadhai is large enough you can make all the "boondis" at once, or you can make them in 2 or 3 batches with a smaller kadhai.

4

When cooked, remove the drops from the kadhai and drain on paper towels. When completely dry, store in a suitable container or plastic bag.

5

Use as and when needed; if to be used gradually, make sure that they are not left in the open for long.

Chapter 2

Chutneys
(Chatniyaan)

Chutneys form an integral part of an Indian meal. A meal is not complete unless there is a relish or chutney of some description on the menu. Chutneys go well with quick meals and snacks, and most of them are suitable for western food, and for picnics and parties. The weather during the summer and rainy months usually wilts the appetite and leaves the digestive powers of the human body at their lowest ebb; chutneys naturally perk up the sluggish taste buds and keep the system going by aiding digestion. They liven up a meal by offering a sharp contrast in flavour and taste; they also provide much-needed vitamins. Indian chutneys are nothing like their western counterparts; they are made at high speed and are sure to please the impatient.

Chutneys can be sour, sweet, or sweet-and-sour; they can be hot and pungent or mild and sweet. Everyday chutneys in India are simple relishes prepared in a variety of ways, but the fresh ones are generally made by grinding herbs, vegetables, and fruits, or dried fruits and nuts. Chutneys can be ground on the traditional sil-batta, or by using the mortar and pestle or an electric grinder. The ground ingredients are then mixed with the seasoning and spices — India is the home of unlimited fragrant spices which can be used in making chutneys. Finally, the needed consistency is obtained by the addition of water, lemon or tamarind juice, or vinegar. Molasses or sugar are added to make a sweet chutney, and a combination of the thinners and sweeteners gives you a choice of sweet-and-sour chutneys.

Chutneys can be expensive when bought ready-made from stores, but they are economical and give you a feeling of achievement when you make them at home. Use the vegetables and fruits in season when they are plentiful and inexpensive. The permutations for making new and unusual chutneys must be limitless; feel free to experiment with your preferred alternative ingredients. That will offer you a sensation of having discovered "new" dishes, and it will no doubt inculcate in you a deeper interest in Indian cuisine. Far be it from me to discourage either!

Most fresh chutneys improve by chilling; they also become more acceptable if they are teamed up imaginatively with the other dishes in the meal, according to their aroma and flavour. Serve chutneys in clear glass or china bowls, or in bowls of contrasting colours; they will thus lend colour to your dining table. Fresh chutneys should normally be made for, and consumed at, each meal; if it is intended for use at the next meal, it should be stored in the refrigerator. Sweet chutneys of the cooked variety can be kept for a few days. However, if a chutney is supposed to last longer than a few days, it is a pickle and not a chutney at all.

SOUR CHUTNEYS

(Khatti Chatniyaan)

BABACO CHUTNEY

(Kamrakh Chatni)

Serves 4

Preparation time 5 minutes plus chilling time

An exotic chutney *par excellence!* A babaco, when ripe, is a large yellow rocket-shaped fruit with soft juicy flesh, which tastes exotically of strawberries and pineapple rolled into one. Although not commonly available, I have seen babacoes sold in many Asian grocery shops from time to time, in London and elsewhere. If the chutney is too thick, add a little water.

Imperial (Metric)	American
4 small, ripe babacoes	4 small, ripe babacoes
20 mint leaves	20 mint leaves
1 fresh green chilli, chopped	1 fresh green chili, chopped
Pinch of white cumin seeds	Dash of white cumin seeds
Pinch of mustard seeds	Dash of mustard seeds
Sea salt to taste	Sea salt to taste
Water as necessary	Water as necessary

1
Top and tail the babacoes, cut up and remove seeds.

2
Put the babacoes, together with mint leaves, green chillies, cumin seeds, mustard seeds, and salt, in a mortar and pound with pestle (or use a sil-batta) into a pulp.

3
Add water to thin the chutney to the desired consistency.

4
Refrigerate and serve as needed.

GREEN MINT CHUTNEY

(Podina Chatni)

Serves 4

Preparation time   5 minutes plus chilling time

This aromatic concoction should please everyone, both by its soothing looks and pungency in taste. Make fresh each time.

Imperial (Metric)	American
2 oz (50g) fresh mint leaves	2 ounces green mint leaves
1 spring onion, chopped	1 scallion, chopped
2 teaspoons fresh pomegranate seeds, whole	2 teaspoons fresh pomegranate seeds, whole
1 green chilli, chopped	1 green chili, chopped
Pinch of white cumin seeds	Dash of white cumin seeds
Sea salt to taste	Sea salt to taste
4 tablespoons lemon juice	⅓ cup lemon juice

1

Place the first 4 ingredients on a sil-batta (or in an electric grinder or mortar and pestle) and grind coarsely.

2

Add the cumin and salt, and grind a little more.

3

Remove the ground mixture and place in a bowl; use some lemon juice to clean out the mixture from the grooves of the sil.

4

Add the rest of the lemon juice and blend.

5

Serve chilled.

ONION CHUTNEY

(Pyaaz Chatni)

Serves 4

Preparation time   10 minutes plus chilling time

Onion is not normally associated with being ground into chutney, but this chutney is one that prescribes just that. Make it and find out what you have been missing! Serve as a side dish.

Imperial (Metric)	American
2 medium onions	2 medium onions
2 medium green peppers	2 medium green peppers
½ teaspoon sliced ginger root	½ teaspoon sliced ginger root
20 fresh mint leaves	20 fresh mint leaves
Pinch of mustard seeds	Dash of mustard seeds
Dash of asafoetida powder	Dash of asafoetida powder
Sea salt to taste	Sea salt to taste
4 tablespoons lemon juice	⅓ cup lemon juice

1

Peel the onions and top and tail the peppers; then chop both.

2

Place together with ginger, mint, mustard, asafoetida, and salt in an electric grinder, and make a thin paste.

3

Remove to a serving dish; add lemon juice and blend.

4

Serve chilled as needed.

WHITE RADISH CHUTNEY

(Chatni Mooli Ki)

Serves 4

Preparation time 5 minutes plus chilling time

White radish is readily available at an Indian market; red radish may be used instead. You may, of course, prefer to mix the two. Any way made, the concoction should delight all chutney lovers.

Imperial (Metric)	American
4 oz (100g) white radish	¼ pound white radish
2 fresh green chillies	2 fresh green chilies
Small pinch of asafoetida powder	Small dash of asofoetida powder
½ teaspoon white cumin seeds	½ teaspoon white cumin seeds
½ teaspoon sliced, fresh ginger	½ teaspoon sliced, fresh ginger
Sea salt to taste	Sea salt to taste
2 tablespoons chopped green coriander	2 tablespoons chopped cilantro (coriander)
4 tablespoons lemon juice	⅓ cup lemon juice

1

Clean and wash the radishes and chillies; scrape the outer skin off the radishes and then chop them and the chillies.

2

Place them, together with the rest of the ingredients, in a blender and switch on for about 20 seconds. Alternatively, use a sil-batta.

3

Remove the chutney to a serving dish.

4

Refrigerate, and serve.

APRICOT CHUTNEY

(Khubaani Chatni)

Serves 4

Preparation time   10 minutes plus chilling time

Use half-ripe apricots for this chutney, and chill before serving. You may also serve it with western foods. As an alternative, you may make a similar chutney with unripe pears.

Imperial (Metric)	American
½ lb (225g) half-ripe apricots	½ pound half-ripe apricots
2 tablespoons chopped green coriander	2 tablespoons chopped cilantro
½ teaspoon sliced ginger root	(coriander)
1 teaspoon chopped onion	½ teaspoon sliced ginger root
1 teaspoon red chilli powder	1 teaspoon chopped onion
Sea salt to taste	1 teaspoon red chili powder
Lemon juice as needed	Sea salt to taste
	Lemon juice as needed

1

Wash and dry the apricots; then halve them and remove the stones.

2

Place in a mortar together with coriander (cilantro), ginger, and onion, and pound with a pestle into a pulp.

3

Stir in the chilli powder and salt, and pound some more.

4

Remove to a serving bowl and add lemon juice if too thick.

5

Refrigerate, and serve.

GREEN TOMATO CHUTNEY

(Chatni Kachche Tamaatar Ki)

Serves   4

Preparation time   10 minutes plus chilling time

A delightful chutney, although it has no claim to fame! The consistency of this chutney can be thick or thin according to your preference; add lemon juice to make it thinner. A good picnic food provided it is not too thin.

Imperial (Metric)	American
4 medium green tomatoes	4 medium green tomatoes
4 spring onions	4 scallions
2 tablespoons chopped green coriander	2 tablespoons chopped cilantro
1 green chilli, chopped	(coriander)
½ teaspoon grated fresh ginger	1 green chili, chopped
Sea salt to taste	½ teaspoon grated fresh ginger
Lemon juice as required	Sea salt to taste
	Lemon juice as required

1

Wash and dry the tomatoes and onions; then chop them up.

2

Place them, together with coriander (cilantro), chilli, ginger, and salt over a "sil", and grind coarsely with the "batta", or use an electric grinder.

3

Remove to a serving dish; add lemon juice as needed if chutney is too thick and lumpy for your taste.

4

Refrigerate before serving.

DRIED MANGO CHUTNEY

(Amchoor Chatni)

Serves 4
Preparation time 5 minutes plus soaking and chilling time

This chutney will be a novelty for western cooks, although in India "amchoor" chutney is well known and is quite popular. Dried mango slices (amchoor) are available at all Indian grocers. Serve as a side dish.

Imperial (Metric)	*American*
2 oz (50g) dried mango slices	2 ounces dried mango slices
20 mint leaves	20 mint leaves
1 fresh green chilli, chopped	1 fresh green chili, chopped
1 clove garlic, sliced	1 clove garlic, sliced
¼ teaspoon grated, fresh ginger	¼ teaspoon grated, fresh ginger
1 teaspoon coriander seeds	1 teaspoon coriander seeds
Sea salt to taste	Sea salt to taste

1

Soak the mango slices in water to cover overnight, or soak in warm water about 2 hours.

2

Place the mango slices, together with the water they were soaking in and the rest of the ingredients, over the "sil", and grind finely with the "batta" (or use an electric grinder).

3

Chill and serve with a meal or savoury snacks.

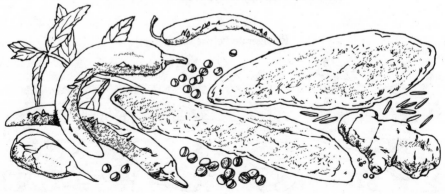

GRAPE CHUTNEY

(Angoor Chatni)

Serves 6

Preparation time 5 minutes plus chilling time

Not a commonly known chutney, but I am sure it will be well liked. Use seedless grapes for this concoction if you can; otherwise grind the seeds also. A piquant chutney which will add a new dimension to a meal!

Imperial (Metric)	American
½ lb (225g) grapes	1 cup grapes
2 tablespoons green coriander	2 tablespoons fresh cilantro
Pinch of white cumin seeds	Dash of white cumin seeds
½ teaspoon sliced ginger root	½ teaspoon sliced ginger root
2 small green chillies, chopped	2 small green chilies, chopped
Lemon juice (optional)	Lemon juice (optional)

1

Wash and dry the grapes and coriander (cilantro).

2

Coarsely grind them, together with the cumin, ginger, chillies, and salt, on a sil-batta or with a mortar and pestle (or use an electric grinder).

3

If the consistency of the chutney is too thick, add lemon juice to make it thinner.

4

Refrigerate before serving.

GREEN LOQUAT CHUTNEY

(Chatni Kachche Lukaat Ki)

Serves   4

Preparation time   5 minutes plus chilling time

A real scoop for lovers of the exotic! Persuade your Indian grocer to obtain some loquats, and a fantastic taste comes to your dining table with this chutney. Serve with any meal or savoury snack.

Imperial (Metric)	American
8 green loquats	8 green loquats
2 oz (50g) mint leaves	2 ounces mint leaves
2 small green chillies, chopped	2 small green chilies, chopped
½ teaspoon white cumin seeds	½ teaspoon white cumin seeds
Sea salt to taste	Sea salt to taste
Water as needed	Water as needed

1

Wash and dry the loquats; then halve them and remove the seeds.

2

Place on a "sil," together with the mint, chillies, cumin, and salt, and using the "batta" grind them coarsely (alternatively use the mortar and pestle or an electric grinder).

3

Add enough water to obtain the desired consistency; then refrigerate for at least 30 minutes.

4

Serve as needed.

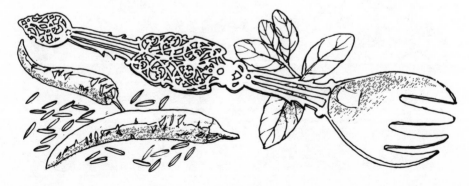

GOOSEBERRY CHUTNEY

(Chatni Karonde Ki)

Serves   6

Preparation time   10 minutes plus chilling time

For best results buy Indian green "karondas" (gooseberries). The consistency of this exotic sour chutney is controlled by the use of water. It is very suitable for picnics and parties; otherwise serve as a side dish.

Imperial (Metric)	American
½ lb (225g) gooseberries	1 cup gooseberries
2 tablespoons chopped green coriander	2 tablespoons chopped cilantro
Pinch of white cumin seeds	(coriander)
1 fresh green chilli, chopped	Dash of of white cumin seeds
Sea salt to taste	1 fresh green chili, chopped
½ teaspoon red chilli powder	Sea salt to taste
Water as needed	½ teaspoon red chili powder
	Water as needed

1

Wash, dry, and halve the gooseberries; then remove their seeds.

2

Place them, together with the coriander (cilantro), cumin, and green chilli, into a mortar and crush with the pestle (or use a sil-batta and grind very coarsely).

3

Add salt and chilli powder, and pound a little more; then add water and blend, bringing the chutney to the desired consistency.

4

Chill before serving.

FRESH CORIANDER CHUTNEY

(Chatni Hara Dhaniyaan)

Serves 6

Preparation time   10 minutes plus chilling time

A freshly made green coriander chutney fills the dining room with an appetizing aroma and is "finger-licking good" in taste. It is very suitable for picnics and parties or with western savoury snacks.

Imperial (Metric)	American
3 spring onions	3 scallions
2 oz (50g) fresh coriander leaves	2 ounces fresh cilantro (coriander)
½ teaspoon chopped fresh ginger	½ teaspoon chopped fresh ginger
2 fresh green chillies	2 fresh green chilies
Sea salt to taste	Sea salt to taste
6 tablespoons lemon juice	½ cup lemon juice

1

Clean and chop the first four ingredients.

2

Grind them coarsely over the sil-batta or in an electric grinder; no water should be added.

3

Add the salt, grind a little more, and remove the contents to a bowl; use a little lemon juice to remove all of the mixture into the bowl.

4

Pour in lemon juice and blend well; chill before serving.

CUMIN SEED CHUTNEY

(Zeere Waali Chatni)

Serves 6
Preparation time   5 minutes plus chilling time

This chutney enhances the taste of kababs and tikkas no end. One of the premier sour chutneys from India, it is made in a jiffy. Serve freshly made, and chilled.

Imperial (Metric)	American
1 tablespoon cumin seeds	1 tablespoon cumin seeds
3 cloves garlic, peeled	3 cloves garlic, peeled
Sea salt to taste	Sea salt to taste
1 dried red chilli, whole	1 dried red chilli, whole
6 tablespoons fresh lemon juice	½ cup fresh lemon juice

1

Place the first 4 ingredients on a sil-batta (alternatively, use an electric grinder or mortar and pestle), and grind very coarsely.

2

Add lemon juice and blend thoroughly.

3

Chill before serving.

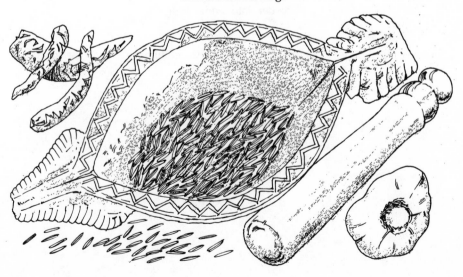

MANGO CHUTNEY

(Chatni Hare Aam Ki)

Serves 6

Preparation time 10 minutes plus chilling time

This is an exotic and refreshing chutney which injects new life into the blandest of meals! Make fresh and serve as a side dish with savoury snacks for a meal. Add a little water if too thick for your liking.

Imperial (Metric)	American
4 small green mangoes	4 small green mangoes
4 tablespoons green coriander	4 tablespoons cilantro (coriander)
1 fresh, green chilli	1 fresh, green chili
Pinch of asafoetida powder	Dash of asafoetida powder
Sea salt to taste	Sea salt to taste
Pinch white cumin seeds	Dash white cumin seeds
½ teaspoon red chilli powder (optional)	½ teaspoon red chili powder (optional)

1

Clean the mangoes; remove the outer skins and stones, if any, and chop up the flesh. Also chop the coriander (cilantro) and the green chilli.

2

Using a sil-batta, coarsely grind all the ingredients together, except for the red chilli powder, into a thick pulp.

3

Remove the chutney to a glass bowl. Sprinkle the chilli powder over the mixture.

4

Chill before serving.

COCONUT CHUTNEY

(Golay ki Chatni)

Serves 4

Preparation time 15 minutes plus chilling time

This chutney is frequently served in tandem with other chutneys or sauces with South Indian dishes. Serve as a side dish with whatever you like.

Imperial (Metric)	American
Large pinch of white cumin seeds, dry-roasted	Large dash of white cumin seeds, dry-roasted
1 tablespoon roasted gram daal	1 tablespoon roasted gram daal
2 tablespoons grated, fresh coconut	2 tablespoons grated, fresh coconut
1 fresh green chilli, chopped	1 fresh green chili, chopped
½ teaspoon sliced fresh ginger	½ teaspoon sliced fresh ginger
Sea salt to taste	Sea salt to taste
4 tablespoons lemon juice	⅓ cup lemon juice

1

Place all the prepared ingredients — from roasted cumin to sliced ginger — in a mortar and crush with a pestle.

2

Add salt and lemon juice, and crush and blend again.

3

Remove to a serving dish, and refrigerate before serving.

GUAVA CHUTNEY

(Amrood Chatni)

Serves 6

Preparation time 10 minutes plus chilling time

Buy fresh, ripe guavas from your Indian grocer; the chutney you make will taste out of this world. Adjust the consistency of the preparation to your liking by using more or less lemon juice. Serve as a side dish.

Imperial (Metric)	American
4 small, ripe guavas	4 small, ripe guavas
2 tablespoons mint leaves	2 tablespoons mint leaves
2 small, fresh chillies	2 small, fresh chilies
½ teaspoon sliced, fresh ginger root	½ teaspoon sliced, fresh ginger root
Sea salt to taste	Sea salt to taste
6 tablespoons lemon juice	½ cup lemon juice

1
Wash and dry the guavas, mint, and chillies; then chop up.

2
Put these, together with ginger and salt, on a "sil", and grind coarsely with the "batta" (or use a grinder of your choice).

3
Remove the thick pulp to a serving bowl, and add lemon juice; blend thoroughly.

4
Chill before serving.

SWEET AND SWEET-AND-SOUR CHUTNEYS

(Meethi aur Khatmitthee Chatniyaan)

SWEET MANGO CHUTNEY

(Aam ki Meethi Chatni)

Serves   4
Preparation time   10 minutes plus chilling time

An exotic preparation to delight your guests; made quickly, this sweet chutney usually has a thick consistency and can be taken with packed lunches and on picnics.

Imperial (Metric)	American
4 medium mangoes, sweet but firm	4 medium mangoes, sweet but firm
1 tablespoon finely chopped mint leaves	1 tablespoon finely chopped mint leaves
Small pinch of asafoetida powder	Small dash of asafoetida powder
½ teaspoon white cumin seeds	½ teaspoon white cumin seeds
Sea salt to taste	Sea salt to taste
½ teaspoon red chilli powder	½ teaspoon red chili powder
1 tablespoon crushed molasses sugar	1 tablespoon crushed molasses sugar

1
Clean and slice the mangoes.

2
Place all the ingredients on a "sil", and grind coarsely with a "batta" (or use a mortar and pestle).

3
Remove to a serving dish. Add a little water if the mixture is too thick and lumpy, and blend.

4
Chill before serving.

PEA POD CHUTNEY

(Chatni Matar Chhilkon ki)

Serves	4
Preparation time	10 minutes
Cooking time	15 minutes

This is a sweet chutney that can be sweet-and-sour if you adjust the quantity of lemon juice. Serve with a meal or with snacks. There is no need to chill before serving.

Imperial (Metric)	American
4 oz (100g) pea pods (but no peas)	¼ pound pea pods (but no peas)
2 teaspoons ghee	2 teaspoons ghee
Pinch of asafoetida powder	Dash of asafoetida powder
Sea salt to taste	Sea salt to taste
1 teaspoon red chilli powder	1 teaspoon red chili powder
1 tablespoon fennel	1 tablespoon fennel
2 oz (50g) raw cane sugar	¼ cup raw sugar
1 tablespoon lemon juice	1 tablespoon lemon juice
½ teaspoon garam masala	½ teaspoon garam masala

1

Wash the pods, and then shred them.

2

Heat the ghee in a saucepan together with asafoetida. After 2 minutes, add shredded pods and stir thoroughly.

3

Stir in the salt, chilli powder, and fennel; cook, stirring, over medium heat for about 2 minutes.

4

Add sugar and cook, stirring, until sugar is melted and blends with the mixture — about 5 to 7 minutes.

5

Stir in lemon juice; sprinkle the garam masala over the mixture, and remove pan from heat. Let cool, and serve as needed.

NOTE: Left-over chutney can be stored in the refrigerator for another day or two.

SWEET TOMATO CHUTN

(Meethi Tamaatar Chatni)

Serves	*4*
Preparation time	*5 minutes*
Cooking time	*10 minutes*

This chutney is delicious. If too sweet, add a little lemon juice. There is no need to chill before serving, but leftovers can go into the refrigerator for no more than a couple of days. A colourful side dish!

Imperial (Metric)	American
4 firm, red tomatoes	4 firm, red tomatoes
2 teaspoons ghee	2 teaspoons ghee
Pinch of asafoetida powder	Dash of asafoetida powder
Sea salt to taste	Sea salt to taste
½ teaspoon red chilli powder	½ teaspoon red chili powder
2 tablespoons raw cane sugar	2 tablespoons raw sugar
2 tablespoons chopped green coriander	2 tablespoons chopped cilantro (coriander)

1
Clean the tomatoes; then chop.

2
Heat the ghee in a saucepan over medium heat. Add the asafoetida and cook, stirring, for about 2 minutes. Stir in the tomatoes, and mix thoroughly.

3
Sprinkle the salt and chilli powder over the mixture, and stir well for 2 to 3 minutes. Then add the sugar and cook, stirring, for about 10 minutes, or until the whole mixture assumes a thick and smooth consistency.

4
Remove pan from heat; stir in the chopped coriander (cilantro) and let the mixture cool.

5
Serve with a meal or with savoury snacks.

PEAR CHUTNEY

(Chatni Naashpaati ki)

Serves	*20 helpings*
Preparation time	*10 minutes*
Cooking time	*30 minutes*

This is another sweet-and-sour chutney which clearly lends itself to experimentation with alternatives. The preparation infuses fresh life even into boiled, bland, and insipid meals!

Imperial (Metric)	*American*
6 ripe, medium pears	6 ripe, medium pears
½ pint (300ml) tamarind juice	1¼ cups tamarind juice
½ lb (225g) raw cane sugar	1 cup raw sugar
Sea salt to taste	Sea salt to taste
1 teaspoon red chilli powder	1 teaspoon red chili powder
2 cloves garlic, sliced	2 cloves garlic, sliced
1 tablespoon chopped onion	1 tablespoon chopped onion
½ teaspoon grated, fresh ginger	½ teaspoon grated, fresh ginger
½ teaspoon garam masala	½ teaspoon garam masala

1

Clean and peel the pears; core and then chop. Put in a saucepan with enough water to cover, and bring to a boil. Remove from heat, and drain off the water.

2

In a separate saucepan, place the tamarind juice and sugar, and bring to a boil over moderate heat. Add the pears, together with all the rest of the ingredients except garam masala, cover the pan, lower heat, and simmer about 15 minutes.

3

Lift off the lid, and sprinkle on the garam masala; replace the lid and remove the pan from heat.

4

Serve when cool. Store what is not immediately needed in a lidded glass jar for later use.

WHITE SESAME CHUTNEY

(Safeid Til ki Chatni)

Serves 4

Preparation time 10 minutes plus soaking and chilling time

You must have heard of sweet and savoury snacks made of sesame seeds, but I am not sure if it is widely known that a delightful sweet-and-sour chutney can also be made from sesame seeds! Make it and give your family and friends a pleasant surprise.

Imperial (Metric)	American
2 oz (50g) white sesame seeds	½ cup white sesame seeds
Sea salt to taste	Sea salt to taste
1 fresh green chilli, chopped	1 fresh green chili, chopped
Small pinch of asafoetida powder	Small dash of asafoetida powder
½ teaspoon white cumin seeds	½ teaspoon white cumin seeds
1 tablespoon raw cane sugar	1 tablespoon raw sugar
2 tablespoons tamarind juice	2 tablespoons tamarind juice
1 tablespoon shredded mint leaves	1 tablespoon shredded mint leaves

1

Clean the sesame seeds, and soak them in warm water about 15 minutes. Then drain off the water, and place the sesame seeds on the "sil."

2

Add salt, chilli, asafoetida, cumin, and sugar and, using the "batta", grind into a fine paste (or use a mortar and pestle).

3

Remove to a serving bowl, and add the tamarind juice and any additional salt and blend thoroughly.

4

Garnish with mint, and refrigerate at least 30 minutes; serve when needed.

CUCUMBER CHUTNEY

(Kheere ki Chatni)

Serves 4
Preparation time   15 minutes plus soaking time
Cooking time   15 minutes

This delectable sweet chutney can also be made with Indian "kakdees" (also known as cucumber in English) if they are available. Serve as an accompaniment to savoury snacks like the pakoda, or with a meal; feel free to serve with western snacks or take on picnics.

Imperial (Metric)	American
4 oz (100g) cucumber	4 ounces cucumber
4 oz (100g) raw cane sugar	½ cup raw sugar
½ pint (300ml) water	1¼ cups water
Sea salt to taste	Sea salt to taste
Small pinch of black salt	Small dash of black salt
1 teaspoon white cumin seeds, roasted and ground	1 teaspoon white cumin seeds, roasted and ground
1 teaspoon grated, fresh ginger	1 teaspoon grated, fresh ginger
1 tablespoon mixture of slivered dry dates and almonds	1 tablespoon mixture of slivered dry dates and almonds
4 tablespoons lemon juice	⅓ cup lemon juice

1

Wash and then peel the cucumber; grate it and soak in water 10 to 15 minutes.

2

Meanwhile, place the sugar and measured water in a saucepan; put over moderate heat and bring to a boil. Remove pan from heat.

3

Squeeze out the cucumber from the soaking water and add to the boiled sugar mixture; add the rest of the ingredients in order of listing and return the pan to moderate heat. Cook another 5 minutes before removing the pan from the heat to let the chutney cool.

4

Serve as needed; store the remainder in the refrigerator or in a covered container. Do not keep it for more than two or three days.

EURO-PRO X ®

TOASTER OVEN
HORNO TOSTADOR
FOUR GRILLE-PAIN

OWNER'S MANUAL
MANUAL DEL USUARIO
GUIDE D'UTILISATION
Model/Modelos/Modèles TO284-TO284L
120 V, 60 Hz, 1200 watts/ vatios

USA: **EURO-PRO Operating LLC**
94 Main Mill Street, Door 16
Plattsburgh, NY 12901

Canada: **EURO-PRO Operating LLC**
4400 Bois Franc
St. Laurent, QC H4S 1A7

Tel.: 1 (800) 798-7398
www.euro-pro.com

IMPORTANT SAFETY INSTRUCTIONS

When using your *Toaster Oven*, basic safety precautions should always be observed, including the following:

1. Read all instructions before using your *Toaster Oven*.
2. Do not touch hot surfaces. Always use handles or knobs.
3. Close supervision is necessary when any appliance is used by or near children.
4. To protect against electric shock, do not immerse cord, plug or any parts of the oven in water or any other liquids.
5. Do not let cord hang over edge of table or counter, or touch hot surfaces.
6. Do not operate appliance with damaged cord or plug or after the appliance malfunctions or has been damage in any manner. Return appliance to the nearest *EURO-PRO Operating LLC* for examination, repair or adjustment.
7. The use of accessory attachments not recommended by the appliance manufacturer may cause hazard or injury.
8. Do not place on or near a hot gas or electric burner.
9. When operating the oven, keep at least four inches of free space on all sides of the oven to allow for adequate air circulation.
10. Unplug from outlet when not in use and before cleaning. Allow to cool before putting on or taking off parts, and before cleaning.
11. To disconnect, turn the time control button to OFF, then remove the plug. Always hold the plug, and never pull the cord.
12. Extreme caution must be used when moving a drip pan containing hot oil or other hot liquids.
13. Do not cover crumb tray or any part of the oven with metal foil. This may cause the oven to overheat.
14. Use extreme caution when removing the tray, racks or disposing of hot grease or other hot liquids.
15. Do not clean the inside of the oven with metal scouring pads. Pieces can break off the pad and touch electrical parts, creating a risk of electric shock.
16. Oversized foods or metal utensils must not be inserted in a toaster oven as they may create a fire or risk of electric shock.
17. A fire may occur if the oven is covered or touching flammable material, including curtains, draperies, walls and the like when in operation. Do not place any items on the oven during operation.
18. Extreme caution should be exercised when using cooking or baking containers constructed of anything other than metal or ovenproof glass.
19. Be sure that nothing touches the top or bottom elements of the oven.
20. Do not place any of the following materials in the oven: cardboard, plastic, paper, or anything similar.
21. Do not store any materials other than manufacturer's recommended accessories in this oven when not in use.
22. This appliance is OFF when the Timer Control button is in the "OFF" position.
23. Always wear protective, insulated oven gloves when inserting or removing items from the hot oven.
24. This appliance has a tempered, safety glass door. The glass is stronger than ordinary glass and more resistant to breakage. Tempered glass can still break around the edges. Avoid scratching door surface or nicking edges.
25. Do not use outdoors.
26. Do not use appliance for other than intended use.

This unit has a short power supply cord to Reduce the risk resulting from becoming entangled in or tripping over a long cord. An extension cord may be used if you are careful in its use:
1. The electrical rating of the extension cord should be at least as great as the electrical rating of the appliance.
2. An extension cord with the power cord must be arranged so that it will not drape over the countertop or tabletop where they can be pulled on by children or tripped over accidentally.

SAVE THESE INSTRUCTIONS
For Household Use Only

WARNING: To reduce the risk of electric shock, this appliance has a polarized plug (one blade is wider than the other). This plug will fit in a polarized outlet only one way. If the plug does not fit fully in the outlet, reverse the plug. If it still does not fit, contact a qualified electrician to install the proper outlet. Do not modify the plug in any way.

Conservez la chaleur des plats cuits jusqu'à 30 minutes. N'excédez pas cette durée : la nourriture séchera et se perdra.

Fonctionnement

- Réglez la température à 180° F.
- Tournez le bouton de fonction à la position « Keep Warm » (réchaud).
- Tournez la minuterie à la position « Stay On » (demeurer en fonction).
- Tournez le bouton de fonctionnement à la position « OFF » (arrêt) lorsque vous avez terminé.

MISE EN GARDE: Lorsque vous retirez des plateaux du four, retenez toujours la grille. Ne lâchez pas le plateau tant qu'il n'est pas bien supporté par la grille.

Entretien et nettoyage

Avertissement: Assurez-vous de débrancher le four et de le laisser refroidir avant le nettoyage.

Afin d'assurer un fonctionnement des plus sécuritaires, maintenez votre four grille-pain exempt de graisse et d'accumulation de nourriture. Nettoyez les parois intérieures à l'aide d'une éponge, d'un linge ou d'un tampon à récurer de nylon humides et d'un savon doux. **N'UTILISEZ PAS DE LAINE D'ACIER NI DE NETTOYANT ABRASIF. NE GRATTEZ PAS LES PAROIS À L'AIDE D'UN USTENSILE DE MÉTAL. CES MÉTHODES POURRAIENT ENDOMMAGER L'APPAREIL.**

Tous les accessoires devraient être lavés à l'eau savonneuse chaude, ou au lave-vaisselle. La porte peut être essuyée à l'aide d'une éponge humide et séchée à l'aide d'une serviette de papier ou de tissu. Nettoyez l'extérieur à l'aide d'une éponge humide. **N'UTILISEZ PAS DE NETTOYANT ABRASIF, PUISQU'IL POURRAIT ENDOMMAGER LA SURFACE EXTERNE.**

N'UTILISEZ PAS DE LAINE D'ACIER OU DE NETTOYANT ABRASIF SUR LA RÔTISSOIRE, PUISQU'ILS POURRAIENT ENDOMMAGER SON ÉMAIL.

LAISSEZ TOUTES LES PIÈCES ET SURFACES SÉCHER COMPLÈTEMENT AVANT DE BRANCHER ET D'UTILISER L'APPAREIL.

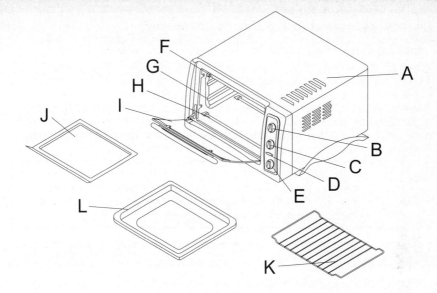

A. Housing
B. Temperature Control
C. Function Control
D. Power ON Light
E. Timer
F. Upper Heating Element
G. Rack Support Guides
H. Lower Heating Element
I. Glass Door
J. Crumb Tray
K. Wire Rack (x2)
L. Bake Tray

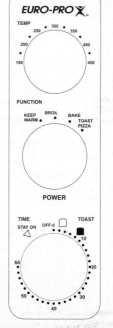

CONTROL PANEL

Technical Specifications

Voltage: 120V., 60Hz.
Power: 1200 Watts

2

Read all the sections of this booklet and follow all the instructions carefully.

Before Using Your Toaster Oven

1. Read all of the instructions included in this manual.
2. Make sure that the oven is unplugged and the Time Control is in the "OFF" position.
3. Wash all the accessories in hot, soapy water or in the dishwasher.
4. Thoroughly dry all accessories and re-assemble in oven. Plug oven into outlet and you are ready to use your new Toaster Oven.
5. After re-assembling your oven, we recommend that you run it at the highest temperature (450° F.) on the Toast Function for approximately 15 minutes to eliminate any packing residue that may remain after shipping. This will also remove all traces of odor initially present.

Please Note: Initial start-up operation may result in minimal smell and smoke (about 15 minutes). This is normal and harmless. It is due to burning of the protective substance applied to the heating elements in the factory.

Using Your Toaster Oven

Please familiarize yourself with the following oven functions and accessories prior to first use:
• **Temperature Control** - Choose the desired temperature from **150°** to **450° F** for baking, broiling, or toasting.
• **Function Control** - This oven is equipped with four positions for a variety of cooking needs:
>   **Bake** - Cakes, pies, cookies, poultry, beef, pork, etc.
>   **Toast/Pizza** - Bread, muffins, frozen waffles, etc.
>   **Broil** - For broiling fish, steak, poultry, pork chops, etc.
>   **Keep Warm** - To keep cooked food warm for up to **30 minutes**.
• **Time Control** - When you turn the control to the left, (counter-clockwise), the oven will "STAY ON" until it is manually shut "OFF". To activate the timer segment of the control, turn to the right (clockwise) to toast or use as a timer. This function also has a bell that rings at the end of the programmed time.
• **Power "On" Light** - It is illuminated whenever the oven is turned on.
• **Bake Tray** - For use in broiling and roasting meat, poultry, fish and various other foods.

WARNING: TO AVOID RISK OF INJURY OR BURNS, DO NOT TOUCH HOT SURFACES WHEN OVEN IS IN USE. ALWAYS USE OVEN MITTS.

Caution: Always use extreme care when removing bake tray, wire rack or any hot container from a hot oven. Always use an oven mitt when removing hot items from the oven.

Broiling

The top heating elements cycle on and off to maintain maximum temperature in the oven. For best results, the oven should be preheated for 20 minutes at 450° before adding the food to be broiled.

Operation

- Set Temperature Control to **450°**.
- Turn Function Control to **Broil.**
- Preheat the oven.
- Place the Wire Rack on the Crumb Tray.
- Place the food on the Wire Rack and slide into the Top Rack Support Guide or Middle Rack Support Guide depending on the thickness of the food that you are cooking.
- Food should be placed as close as possible to the Top Heating Element without touching it.
- Set temperature control to the appropriate temperature.
- Brush food with sauces or oil, as desired.
- Turn Time Control to position **"Stay On"**.
- It is advisable to leave the door **slightly ajar.**
- When broiling is complete, turn the Time Control to **"OFF"**.

Broiling Guide

Cooking results may vary depending on thickness of food being broiled, adjust these times to your individual requirements. Also, remember to turn the meat/fish over halfway through the cooking time and to check often during broiling to avoid overcooking.

MEAT	OVEN TEMP	COOKING TIME
RIB STEAK	400	20-25 min.
T-BONE STEAK	400	20-25 min.
HAMBURGER	400	15-25 min.
PORK CHOPS	400	25-35 min.
LAMB CHOPS	400	30-40 min.
CHICKEN LEGS	400	25-35 min.
FISH FILETS	350	15-25 min.
SALMON STEAKS	350	15-25 min.

Note: All broiling times are based on meats at refrigerator temperature. Frozen meats may take considerably longer. Therefore, use of a meat thermometer is highly recommended.

Baking

Bake your favorite cookies, cakes, pies, brownies, etc. The bake ware that will fit in your oven are up to 9 inches in length. We do not recommend the use of oven roasting bags or glass containers in the oven. **Never** use plastic, cardboard, paper or anything similar in the oven.

Note: Position the wire rack in the lowest Support Guide.

Operation

• Place the wire rack in the **lowest or middle** Rack Support Guide depending on the height of the pan or according to the recipe.
• Place pan with item(s) to be baked on the wire rack.
• Turn the Function Control to **Bake.**
• Turn the Time Control to position **"Stay On".**
• When baking is complete, turn the Time Control to **"OFF".**

Positioning of the Wire Rack

Cookies - Use bottom and middle Support Guides.
Layer Cakes - Use bottom Support Guide only (bake one at a time).
Pies - Use bottom Support Guide.

Baking Cookies

For baking cookies, we suggest adjusting baking temperature and using a cookie sheet placed on the wire rack. Also, using parchment paper on a cookie sheet might prove helpful when baking certain types of cookies.

1. Use parchment paper on cookie sheet so cookies will not stick.
2. Cookie sheets, baking times and temperatures may differ from those necessary when using other baking materials.

Baking Guide

Follow the package or recipe instructions for baking times and temperature.

Recommended Pan Sizes

The following recommended pan sizes should fit your Toaster Oven. To be sure pan will fit, place the pan inside the oven to check before preparing your recipe.
6 - cup muffin pan
8 x 4 loaf pan
9 x 5 loaf pan
8" round or square baking pan or dish
1-1 1/2 quart casserole dish - most types
When baking in loaf pans, we recommend you do not fill more than half full.

Toasting

Large capacity oven allows for toasting 4 to 6 slices of bread, 6 muffins, frozen waffles or frozen pancakes. When toasting only 1 or 2 items, place food on the Wire Rack in the center of the oven.

Operation

- Set the Temperature Control to 450°.
- Turn the Function Control to **Toast**.
- Place food to be toasted on the Wire Rack.
- Ensure Crumb Tray is in place.
- Turn the Time Control to desired darkness. (Light to Dark).
- Bell will ring to signal the end of the Toast cycle.

Note: Wire Rack should be positioned in the middle of the oven with the indentations pointing down.

Toast Settings:

Light: 4 min.
Medium: 7 min.
Dark: 9 min.

CAUTION: When toasting, do not leave food in for longer periods of time other than what is listed above. Toasting for longer than recommended times will burn food.

Keep Warm

Keep cooked food warm for up to 30 minutes. Longer periods of time are not recommended as food will become dry or will spoil.

Operation

- Set the Temperature Control to 180°.
- Turn the Function Control to Keep Warm.
- Turn the Time Control to "Stay On" position.
- Turn the Time Control to "Off" position when finished with Keep Warm.

CAUTION: **When sliding trays out of oven, always support the rack. Do not let go until you are sure the rack is securely supported.**

Care & Cleaning

Warning: **Be sure to unplug the oven and allow it to cool before cleaning.**

To assure maximum safe operation, keep your toaster oven free of grease and build-up of food particles. Clean the inside of the walls with a damp sponge, cloth or nylon scouring pad and mild detergent. **DO NOT USE STEEL WOOL SCOURING PADS, ABRASIVE CLEANERS OR SCRAPE THE WALLS WITH A METAL UTENSIL, AS ALL OF THESE METHODS MAY DAMAGE THE FINISH.**

All accessories should be washed in hot soapy water or can be cleaned in a dishwasher. The door can be wiped with a damp sponge and wiped dry with a paper or cloth towel. Clean the outside with a damp sponge. **DO NOT USE AN ABRASIVE CLEANER AS IT MAY DAMAGE THE EXTERIOR FINISH.**

DO NOT USE AN ABRASIVE CLEANER OR STEEL WOOL SCOURING PAD ON THE BAKE TRAY AS IT MAY DAMAGE THE PORCELAIN ENAMEL FINISH.

LET ALL PARTS AND SURFACES DRY THOROUGHLY PRIOR TO PLUGGING OVEN IN AND USING.

EURO-PRO X

ONE (1) YEAR LIMITED WARRANTY

EURO-PRO Operating LLC warrants this product to be free from defects in material and workmanship for a period of one (1) year from the date of the original purchase, when utilized for normal household use, subject to the following conditions, exclusions and exceptions.

If your appliance fails to operate properly while in use under normal household conditions within the warranty period, return the complete appliance and accessories, freight prepaid to

In U.S.:   **EURO-PRO Operating LLC**, 94 Main Mill Street, Door 16, Plattsburg, N.Y. 12901
In Canada: **EURO-PRO Operating LLC**, 4400 Bois Franc, St. Laurent, Quebec H4S 1A7

If the appliance is found by **EURO-PRO** to be defective in material or workmanship, **EURO-PRO** will repair or replace it free of charge. Proof of purchase date and $ 18.95 to cover the cost of return shipping and handling must be included. *

The liability of **EURO-PRO Operating LLC** is limited solely to the cost of the repair or replacement of the unit at our option. This warranty does not cover normal wear of parts and does not apply to any unit that has been tampered with or used for commercial purposes. This limited warranty does not cover damage caused by misuse, abuse, negligent handling or damage due to faulty packaging or mishandling in transit. This warranty does not cover damage or defects caused by or resulting from damages from shipping or repairs, service or alterations to the product or any of its parts, which have been performed by a repair person not authorized by **EURO-PRO**.

This warranty is extended to the original purchaser of the unit and excludes all other legal and/or conventional warranties. The responsibility of **EURO-PRO Operating LLC** if any, is limited to the specific obligations expressly assumed by it under the terms of the limited warranty. **In no event** is **EURO-PRO Operating LLC** liable for incidental or consequential damages of any nature whatsoever. Some states/provinces do not permit the exclusion or limitation of incidental or consequential damages, so the above may not apply to you.

This warranty gives you specific legal rights, and you may also have other rights which vary from state to state or province to province.

*Important: Carefully pack item to avoid damage in shipping. Be sure to include proof of purchase date and to attach tag to item before packing with your name, complete address and phone number with a note giving purchase information, model number and what you believe is the problem with item. We recommend you insure the package (as damage in shipping is not covered by your warranty). Mark the outside of your package "ATTENTION CUSTOMER SERVICE". We are constantly striving to improve our products, therefore the specifications contained herein are subject to change without notice.

PRODUCT REGISTRATION CARD
FOR CANADIAN CONSUMERS ONLY

Please fill out and mail the product registration card within ten (10) days of purchase. The registration will enable us to contact you in the unlikely event of a product safety notification. By returning this card you acknowledge to have read and understood the instructions for use, and warnings set forth in the accompanying instructions.

RETURN TO EURO-PRO Operating LLC, 4400 Bois Franc, St-Laurent, Qc, H4S 1A7

Model TO284/TO284L

Appliance model

Date purchased   Name of store

Owner's name

Address   City   Prov.   Postal Code

INSTRUCCIONES IMPORTANTES DE SEGURIDAD

Al usar su *Horno Tostador*, siempre debe seguir precauciones básicas de seguridad, incluyendo las siguientes:

1. Lea todas las instrucciones antes de utilizar su *Horno Tostador*.
2. No toque las superficies calientes. Utilice siempre las asas o perillas.
3. Tenga mucho cuidado al utilizar cualquier aparato eléctrico cerca de niños.
4. Para evitar una descarga eléctrica, no sumerja el cable o el enchufe en agua o cualquier otro líquido.
5. No permita que el cable cuelgue sobre el borde de la mesa o mesada, o que toque superficies calientes.
6. No utilice ningún artefacto si el cable o el enchufe están dañados o luego de una falla, o si ha sufrido cualquier tipo de daño. Retórnelo a *EURO-PRO Operating LLC* para que sea examinado, reparado o ajustado.
7. El uso de accesorios no recomendados por el fabricante puede ocasionar peligros o daños.
8. No lo coloque sobre o cerca de un quemador a gas o eléctrico.
9. Al utilizar el horno, mantenga por lo menos cuatro pulgadas de espacio libre en todos los costados del horno para permitir la circulación adecuada del aire.
10. Desenchúfelo del tomacorriente cuando no lo utilice y antes de limpiarlo. Deje que se enfríe antes de ponerle o quitarle partes, y antes de limpiarlo.
11. Para desconectarlo, gire el control de tiempo a OFF, luego desenchúfelo. Siempre sostenga el enchufe, nunca jale del cable.
12. Debe tener mucho cuidado al mover una bandeja que contenga aceite u otros líquidos calientes.
13. No cubra la bandeja de las migas o cualquier otra parte del horno con papel metálico. Esto puede hacer que el horno se recaliente.
14. Tenga mucho cuidado al remover la bandeja, los estantes o al desechar grasa caliente o cualquier otro líquido caliente.
15. No limpie el interior del horno con almohadillas metálicas. Algunas partes pueden romper la almohadilla y hacer que toque partes eléctricas, creando un riesgo de descarga eléctrica.
16. No debe introducir alimentos demasiado grandes o utensilios de metal dentro del horno ya que podrían originar un incendio o el riesgo de una descarga eléctrica.
17. Se podría originar un incendio si el horno está tocando materiales inflamables, incluyendo cortinados, ropas, paredes u otros similares mientras está funcionando. No coloque nada en el horno cuando esté encendido.
18. Debe tener mucho cuidado al utilizar recipientes para cocinar u hornear de cualquier otro material que no sea metal o vidrio apto para horno.
19. Asegúrese de que nada entre en contacto con los elementos superiores e inferiores del horno.
20. No coloque ninguno de los siguientes materiales en el horno: cartón, plástico, papel o similares.
21. No guarde ningún material que no sea los accesorios recomendados por el fabricante en el horno cuando no lo use.
22. Este artefacto está APAGADO cuando la perilla del Control de Tiempo está en la posición "OFF".
23. Use siempre guantes protectores, aislantes para horno al colocar o remover objetos calientes del horno.
24. Este artefacto tiene una puerta de vidrio templado de seguridad. Este vidrio es más fuerte que el vidrio común y más resistente a las roturas. Sin embargo, puede llegar a romperse en los bordes. Evite rayar la superficie de la puerta o golpear sus bordes.
25. No lo utilice en el exterior.
26. No utilice el artefacto para ningún otro uso distinto al indicado.

Esta unidad tiene un cable de alimentación corto para reducir el riesgo de enredarse o tropezarse con un cable más largo. Un cable de extensión puede utilizarse con cuidado:

1. La capacidad eléctrica del cable de extensión debe ser por lo menos igual al consumo del artefacto.
2. No debe permitir que el cable de extensión cuelgue de la mesada o mesa de tal forma que pueda ser jalado por niños o causar que alguien se tropiece.

CONSERVE ESTAS INSTRUCCIONES
Para Uso Doméstico Solamente

ADVERTENCIA: Para reducir el riesgo de una descarga eléctrica, este artefacto posee un enchufe polarizado (una pata es más ancha que la otra). Este enchufe entra completamente en un tomacorriente polarizado en una sola posición. De no ser así, inviértalo, y si aún así no entra completamente, llame a un electricista calificado para que instale un tomacorriente apropiado. No intente modificar el enchufe de ninguna manera.

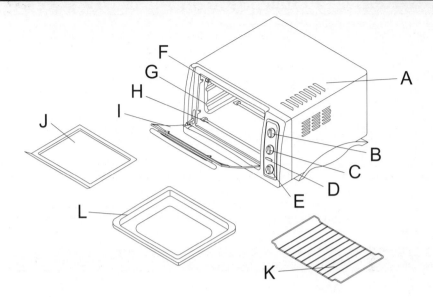

A. Gabinete
B. Control de Temperatura
C. Control de Función
D. Luz de Encendido
E. Temporizador
F. Elemento Calefactor Superior
G. Guías de Soporte para el Estante
H. Elemento Calefactor Inferior
I. Puerta de Vidrio
J. Bandeja para las migas
K. Estante de Alambre (x2)
L. Bandeja

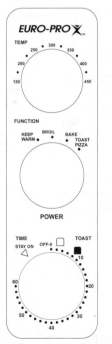

PANEL DE CONTROL

Especificaciones Técnicas
Voltaje: 120V., 60Hz.
Potencia: 1200 Vatios

Lea todas las secciones de este manual y siga todas las instrucciones cuidadosamente.

Antes de Utilizar su Horno Tostador

1. Lea todas las instrucciones de este manual.
2. Verifique que el horno esté desenchufado y que el control de tiempo esté en la posición "OFF".
3. Lave todos los accesorios con agua caliente jabonosa o en el lava vajillas.
4. Seque completamente todos los accesorios y vuelva a colocarlos en el horno. Enchufe el horno y ya está listo para usar su nuevo Horno Tostador.
5. Luego de armar su horno, le recomendamos hacerlo funcionar a la temperatura más alta (450° F) en el modo tostador por unos 15 minutos para eliminar cualquier resto de material de empaque que haya podido quedar. Esto también quitará cualquier olor que pudiera estar presente al principio.

Observaciones: La primera operación puede generar un poco de olor y humo (unos 15 minutos). Esto es normal e inofensivo. Es originado por el quemado de la sustancia protectora que se coloca sobre los elementos calefactores al fabricarlos.

Uso de su Horno Tostador

Debe familiarizarse con las siguientes funciones y accesorios del horno antes de usarlo:
- **Control de temperatura** – Escoja la temperatura deseada desde **150°** a **450° F** para cocinar, hornear, tostar o asar.
- **Control de Función** – Este horno viene con cuatro posiciones para cubrir todas las necesidades de cocción:
  Bake – Tortas, pasteles, galletas, aves, carne, cerdo, etc.
  Toast/Pizza – Pan, muffins, waffles congelados, etc.
  Broil – Para asar pescado, bifes, aves, chuletas de cerdo, etc.
  Keep Warm – Para mantener la comida cocida caliente hasta **30 minutos**.
- **Control de Tiempo** – Cuando gira el control hacia la izquierda (sentido contra horario), el horno permanecerá encendido (Stay On) hasta que lo apague manualmente. Para activar el temporizador, gírelo hacia la derecha (sentido horario) para tostar o para usarlo como temporizador.
  Esta función también tiene una campana que suena al terminar el tiempo programado.
- **Luz de Encendido** – Se ilumina siempre que el horno esté en funcionamiento.
- **Bandeja** - Para cocinar carnes, aves, pescado y otras comidas.

ADVERTENCIA: PARA EVITAR EL RIESGO DE HERIDAS O QUEMADURAS, NO TOQUE LAS SUPERFICIES CALIENTES CUANDO EL HORNO ESTÉ ENCENDIDO. USE SIEMPRE GUANTES PARA HORNO.

Advertencia: Tenga siempre mucho cuidado al quitar la bandeja, el estante de alambre o cualquier otro recipiente del horno caliente. Use siempre un guante para horno al quitar objetos calientes del horno.

El elemento calefactor superior se enciende y apaga para mantener la temperatura máxima del horno. Par obtener mejores resultados, debe precalentar el horno por 20 minutos a 450° antes de agregarle los alimentos a asar.

Operación

Ajuste el control de temperatura a 450°.
Gire el control de funciones a Broil.
Precaliente el horno.
Coloque el estante de alambre sobre la bandeja para las migas.

Coloque los alimentos en el estante de alambre y colóquelo en el soporte de arriba o en el del medio dependiendo del espesor de los alimentos que esté cocinando.

Los alimentos deben colocarse lo más cerca posible del elemento calefactor superior sin llegar a tocarlo.
Ajuste el control de temperatura como lo desee.
Recubra los alimentos con salsas o aceite, si lo desea.
Gire el Control de Tiempo a la posición "Stay On".
Le recomendamos dejar la puerta levemente abierta.
Una vez que haya terminado de cocinar, gire el control de tiempo a "OFF".

Guía de Asado

Los resultados pueden variar dependiendo del grosor de los alimentos a asar, ajuste estos tiempos a sus necesidades particulares. Además, recuerde dar vuelta la carne/pescado en la mitad del tiempo de cocción y verifique a menudo durante la cocción para evitar que se queme.

CARNE	TEMPERATURA DEL HORNO	TIEMPO DE COCCIÓN
BIFE DE COSTILLA	400	20-25 min.
CHULETA	400	20-25 min.
HAMBURGUESAS	400	15-25 min.
CHULETAS DE CERDO	400	25-35 min.
CORDERO	400	30-40 min.
PATAS DE POLLO	400	25-35 min.
FILETE DE PESCADO	350	15-25 min.
BIFES DE SALMÓN	350	15-25 min.

Nota: Todos los tiempos de cocción están basados en las carnes a temperaturas de heladera. Las carnes congeladas pueden tardar mucho más. Por lo tanto, le recomendamos usar un termómetro para carnes.

Hornee sus galletas favoritas, tortas, pasteles, brownies, etc. Puede colocar recipientes de hasta 9 pulgadas de largo en su horno. No le recomendamos utilizar bolsas para hornear o recipientes de vidrio en su horno. **Nunca** utilice plástico, cartón, papel o algo similar en el horno.

Nota: Coloque el estante de alambre en las guías más bajas.

Operación

- Coloque el estante de alambre en la posición **más baja o en el medio**, dependiendo de la altura de la bandeja o de las indicaciones de la receta.
- Coloque la bandeja con los elementos a hornear en el estante de alambre.
- Gire el Control de Funciones a **Bake**.
- Gire el Control de Tiempo a la posición "**Stay On**".
- Una vez que haya terminado de cocinar, gire el control de tiempo a "**OFF**".

Posición del estante de alambre

Galletas – Use la posición más baja o la del medio.
Pasteles de Capas - Use la posición más baja únicamente (hornee una por vez).
Tortas - Use la posición más baja.

Horneado de Galletas

Para hornear galletas, le recomendamos ajustar la temperatura del horno y colocar una bandeja para galletas sobre el estante de alambre. También, es conveniente utilizar papel manteca sobre la bandeja al hornear ciertos tipos de galletas.

1. Use papel manteca sobre la bandeja para que no se peguen las galletas.
2. Las bandejas de galletas, tiempos de cocción y temperatura pueden variar al utilizar otros materiales de horneado.

Guía de Horneado

Siga las instrucciones del paquete o la receta con respecto al tiempo y temperatura de horneado.

Tamaños de Fuentes Recomendados

Los siguientes tamaños recomendados de fuentes entrarán es su Horno Tostador. Para asegurarse de que la fuente entrará en el horno, colóquela en el horno antes de preparar la receta.

Bandeja para muffins de 6 unidades
Bandeja de 8 x 4
Bandeja de 9 x 5
Plato o bandeja redonda o cuadrada de 8"
Cacerola de 1-11/2 litros – casi todas
Al hornear en bandejas, le recomendamos no llenarlas más de la mitad.

Tostador (Toast)

La gran capacidad del horno permite tostar de 4 a 6 rodajas de pan, 6 muffins, waffles o crepés congelados. Al tostar solo 1 o 2 artículos, colóquelos en el estante de alambre en el centro del horno.

Operación
- Ajuste el control de temperatura a 450°.
- Gire el Control de Funciones a **Toast** (tostar).
- Coloque los alimentos a tostar en el estante de alambre.
- Verifique que la bandeja para las migas esté en su lugar.
- Gire el control de tiempo al tostado deseado. (Ligero u Oscuro).
- Sonará una campana para indicarle la finalización del ciclo de tostado.

Nota: El estante de alambre debe colocarse en el medio del horno con las hendiduras apuntando hacia abajo.

Tiempos para el Tostador:
Ligero: 4 min.
Mediano: 7 min.
Oscuro: 9 min.

CUIDADO: Al tostar, no deje los alimentos en el horno por tiempos mayores a los indicados más arriba. El tostarlos por tiempos mayores a los recomendados los quemará.

Mantiene la comida cocida caliente por hasta 30 minutos. No se recomiendan períodos más largos ya que la comida se secará o arruinará.

Operación

- Ajuste el control de temperatura a 180°.
- Gire el Control de Funciones a Keep Warm (Mantener Caliente).
- Gire el Control de Tiempo a la posición "Stay On".
- Gire el Control de Tiempo a la posición "Off" (apagado) cuando termine de usar la función "Keep Warm".

CUIDADO: **Al deslizar las bandejas hacia afuera del horno, sostenga siempre el estante. No lo suelte hasta que esté seguro de que el estante esté sostenido adecuadamente.**

Cuidado y Limpieza

Advertencia: Asegúrese de desenchufar el horno y dejarlo enfriar antes de limpiarlo.

Para obtener una operación segura, mantenga su horno tostador libre de grasa y acumulación de restos de comida. Limpie las paredes con una esponja húmeda, trapo o almohadilla de nylon y con un detergente suave. **NO UTILICE ALMOHADILLAS DE LANA DE ACERO, LIMPIADORES ABRASIVOS O RASPE LAS PAREDES CON UTENSILIOS METÁLICOS, YA QUE TODOS ESTOS MÉTODOS PUEDEN DAÑAR LA TERMINACIÓN.**

Todos los accesorios deben lavarse con agua caliente jabonosa o pueden lavarse en el lavavajillas. La puerta puede repasarse con una esponja húmeda y secarse con una toalla de papel o de tela. Limpie el exterior con una esponja húmeda. **NO UTILICE UN LIMPIADOR ABRASIVO YA QUE PUEDE DAÑAR LA TERMINACIÓN EXTERNA.**

NO UTILICE LIMPIADORES ABRASIVOS O ALMOHADILLAS DE LANA DE ACERO PARA LIMPIAR LA BANDEJA YA QUE PUEDEN DAÑAR LA TERMINACIÓN DE ESMALTE DE PORCELANA.

PERMITA QUE TODAS LAS PARTES Y SUPERFICIES SE SEQUEN COMPLETAMENTE ANTES DE VOLVER A ENCHUFAR Y USAR EL HORNO.

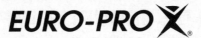

GARANTÍA LIMITADA DE UN (1) AÑO

EURO-PRO Operating LLC garantiza este producto contra defectos de materiales y mano de obra por un término de un (1) año a partir de la fecha de compra original, siempre que sea utilizado para uso doméstico normal, sujeto a las siguientes condiciones, exclusiones y excepciones.

Si su artefacto no funciona correctamente al utilizarlo bajo condiciones domésticas normales dentro del período de garantía, devuelva el artefacto completo y los accesorios, pagando el envío, a:

En los EE.UU.: **EURO-PRO Operating LLC**, 94 Main Mill Street, Door 16, Plattsburgh, N.Y. 12901
En Canadá: **EURO-PRO Operating LLC**, 4400 Bois Franc, St. Laurent, Quebec H4S 1A7

Si EURO-PRO determina que el artefacto presenta un defecto de materiales o mano de obra, lo reparará o remplazará sin cargo. El envío debe incluir un comprobante de la fecha de compra y $18.95 para cubrir los gastos de envío. *

La responsabilidad de **EURO-PRO Operating LLC** se limita únicamente al costo de reparación o reemplazo de la unidad, a nuestro criterio. Esta garantía no cubre el desgaste normal de las partes y no cubre ninguna unidad que haya sido alterada o utilizada con fines comerciales. Esta garantía limitada no cubre daños ocasionados por uso inadecuado, abuso, negligencia o daños causados por embalaje inapropiado o maltrato durante el transporte. Esta garantía no cubre daños o defectos causados o resultantes durante el transporte para su reparación o alteraciones del producto o cualquiera de sus partes, realizadas por una persona no autorizada por EURO-PRO.

Esta garantía es válida para el comprador original del producto y excluye cualquier otra garantía legal y/o convencional. La responsabilidad de **EURO-PRO Operating LLC**, de existir, se limita a las obligaciones específicas asumidas expresamente bajo los términos de esta garantía limitada. Bajo ninguna circunstancia **EURO-PRO Operating LLC** será responsable por daños incidentales o indirectos de ninguna clase. Algunos estados/provincias no permiten la exclusión o limitación de daños consiguientes o incidentales, por lo tanto lo anterior puede no ser válido para usted.

Esta garantía le otorga derechos legales específicos, y usted puede también tener otros derechos los que varían de estado a estado o de provincia a provincia.

*Importante: Embale el producto cuidadosamente para evitar daños durante el transporte. Asegúrese de incluir un comprobante de la fecha de compra y de colocarle una etiqueta al producto con su nombre, dirección completa y número de teléfono, una nota proporcionando información de la compra, número de modelo y una descripción del problema. Le recomendamos asegurar el paquete (puesto que la garantía no cubre daños de envío). Escriba en el exterior del paquete "ATTENTION CUSTOMER SERVICE". Nosotros nos esforzamos constantemente en mejorar nuestros productos, por lo tanto las especificaciones aquí indicadas pueden cambiar sin previo aviso.

TARJETA DE REGISTRO DEL PRODUCTO

SÓLO PARA CONSUMIDORES CANADIENSES

Complete y envíe la tarjeta de registro del producto dentro de los diez (10) días posteriores a la compra. El registro nos permitirá contactarnos con usted en caso de existir alguna notificación de seguridad con respecto al producto. Retornando esta tarjeta usted reconoce haber leído y entendido las instrucciones de uso y advertencias incluidas en estas instrucciones.

ENVÍELO A EURO-PRO Operating LLC, 4400 Bois Franc, St. Laurent, Quebec H4S 1A7

Modelo TO284/TO284L

Modelo del Artefacto

Fecha de compra   **Nombre del Negocio**

Nombre del Usuario

Dirección   Ciudad   Provincia   Código Postal

CONSIGNES DE SÉCURITÉ IMPORTANTES

Lors de l'utilisation de votre *Four grille-pain* , des précautions élémentaires doivent être observées:

1. Lisez toutes les directives avant d'utiliser votre *four grille-pain*.
2. Ne touchez pas aux surfaces chaudes. Utilisez toujours les poignées.
3. Une surveillance attentive est nécessaire lorsque tout appareil est utilisé par des enfants ou à proximité.
4. Pour éviter les risques d'électrocution, évitez d'immerger l'appareil, son cordon, sa fiche ou tout autre composant.
5. Ne laissez pas le cordon traîner sur le dessus d'une table ou d'un comptoir. Ne le laissez pas entrer en contact avec des surfaces chaudes.
6. N'utilisez pas l'appareil si l'appareil, sa fiche ou son cordon sont endommagés, ou si l'appareil ne fonctionne pas correctement. Retournez l'appareil à *EURO-PRO Operating LLC* pour vérification, réparation ou réglage.
7. L'utilisation d'accessoires non recommandés par le fabricant peuvent entraîner des accidents ou causer des blessures.
8. Ne placez pas l'appareil sur ou près d'un brûleur au gaz ou électrique.
9. Lorsque utilisez le four, laissez un espace libre d'au moins quatre pouces de chaque côté du four afin d'assurer une circulation d'air adéquate.
10. Débranchez lorsque vous ne l'utilisez pas et avant de le nettoyer. Laissez l'appareil refroidir avant de le nettoyer ou d'y insérer ou d'en retirer toute pièce.
11. Pour débrancher, mettez le bouton de fonctionnement à la position « OFF » et retirez la fiche de la prise. Tenez toujours la fiche et ne tirez jamais sur le cordon.
12. Soyez extrêmement prudent lorsque vous déplacez une casserole contenant de l'huile ou d'autres liquides chauds.
13. Ne recouvrez aucune pièce du four de papier d'aluminium. Ceci pourrait faire surchauffer le four.
14. Soyez extrêmement prudent lorsque vous retirez le plateau ou les grilles ou lorsque vous jetez de la graisse ou autres liquides chauds.
15. Ne nettoyez pas l'intérieur du four avec de la laine d'acier. Des morceaux pourraient se séparer de la laine et toucher aux composants électriques, augmentant le risque d'électrocution.
16. L'insertion d'ustensile de grand format ou de métal dans le grille-pain peut causer un incendie ou une électrocution.
17. Un incendie peut se produire si le four est couvert ou s'il est en contact avec des produits inflammables, tels que les rideaux, tapisseries, murs, etc., pendant qu'il est en fonction. Ne déposez aucun article sur le four pendant qu'il fonctionne.
18. Soyez extrêmement prudent lorsque vous utilisez des contenants ou des ustensiles faits de matériaux autres que le métal ou le verre résistant à la cuisson.
19. Assurez-vous que rien n'est en contact avec les éléments supérieur ou inférieur du four.
20. Ne déposez aucun des produits suivants dans le four : carton, plastique, papier, ou autre produit semblable.
21. Lorsque le four n'est pas en fonction, n'y rangez aucun produit autre que les accessoires recommandés par le fabricant.
22. Cet appareil est ÉTEINT lorsque le bouton de fonctionnement est à la position « OFF ».
23. Portez toujours des gants de protection isolants pour insérer ou retirer des articles du four lorsqu'il est chaud..
24. Cet appareil est doté d'une porte de sécurité de verre trempé. Ce verre est plus résistant que le verre ordinaire et risque moins de se casser. Le verre trempé peut toutefois se casser près des bords. Évitez de gratter la surface de la porte ou d'entailler les bords.
25. N'utilisez pas l'appareil à l'extérieur.
26. N'utilisez l'appareil qu'à ce pour quoi il a été conçu.

Cet appareil est doté d'un cordon d'alimentation court afin de réduire les risque de s'emmêler dans le cordon ou de trébucher. Une rallonge doit être utilisée avec prudence :
1. La valeur nominale de la rallonge doit être égale ou supérieure à la valeur nominale de l'appareil.
2. La rallonge et le cordon d'alimentation doivent être placés de façon à ne pas tomber par-dessus le comptoir ou la table, afin d'éviter de trébucher et afin de le garder hors de la portée des enfants.

CONSERVEZ CES INSTRUCTIONS
Pour usage domestique seulement

AVERTISSEMENT: Afin de réduire les risques de choc électrique, cet appareil est doté d'un cordon à fiche polarisée (une lame est plus large que l'autre). Cette fiche ne s'insère que dans un seul sens dans une prise polarisée. Si la fiche ne s'insère pas dans la prise, retournez la fiche. Si elle ne s'adapte toujours pas, contactez un électricien qualifié afin d'installer la prise appropriée. N'altérez la fiche d'aucune façon.

FAMILIARISEZ-VOUS AVEC VOTRE FOUR GRILLE-PAIN

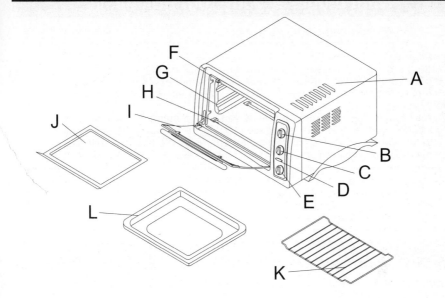

A. Boîtier
B. Réglage de température
C. Réglage de la fonction
D. Témoin d'alimentation
E. Minuterie
F. Élément chauffant supérieur
G. Porte-grille
H. Élément chauffant inférieur
I. Porte de verre
J. Plateau à miettes
K. Grille (x2)
L. Lèchefrite

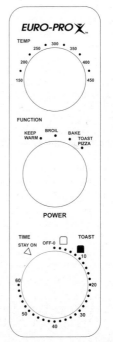

PANNEAU DE CONTRÔLE

Spécifications techniques

Tension :   120 V, 60 Hz
Intensité :   1200 watts

Lisez toutes les sections de ce guide et suivez attentivement toutes les instructions.

Avant d'utiliser votre four grille-pain

1. Lisez toutes les instructions de ce guide.
2. Assurez-vous que le four est débranché et que le bouton de minuterie est à la position « OFF » (arrêt).
3. Nettoyez tous les accessoires à l'eau savonneuse chaude ou au lave-vaisselle.
4. Séchez complètement tous les accessoires et remettez-les dans le four. Branchez le four à l'alimentation. Vous êtes prêt à utiliser votre nouveau four grille-pain.
5. Après l'assemblage de votre four, nous vous recommandons de le faire fonctionner à la température maximale (450° F) de la fonction de grille-pain durant environ 15 minutes afin d'éliminer tout résidu d'emballage suite au transport. Ceci éliminera en autre toute trace d'odeur initiale.

> **Remarque:** Le démarrage initial peut causer une odeur et une fumée minimale durant environ 15 minutes. Ceci est normal et sans danger. Ce phénomène est causé par le brûlage de l'enduit protecteur appliqué aux éléments chauffants en usine.

Utilisation de votre four grille-pain

Veuillez vous familiariser avec les fonctions et les accessoires suivants de votre four avant sa première utilisation :
- **Réglage de température** - Choisissez la température désirée entre **150°F** et **450° F** pour la cuisson, ou le grille-pain.
- **Commande de fonction** - Ce four est doté de quatre positions pour combler divers besoins de cuisson :
  Cuisson - Gâteaux, tartes, biscuits, volaille, boeuf, porc, etc.
  Toast/Pizza (grille-pain)- Pain, muffins, gaufres surgelées, etc.
  Broil - Poisson, steak, volaille, côtelettes de porc, etc.
  Keep Warm (réchaud) - Conservez la chaleur des plats cuits **jusqu'à 30 minutes**.
- **Minuterie** - Lorsque vous tournez la commande vers la gauche (sens antihoraire), le four demeure en fonction (« STAY ON ») jusqu'à ce qu'il soit éteint manuellement (« OFF »). Pour activer la minuterie, tournez le bouton vers la droite (sens horaire) pour le grille-pain ou la minuterie. Cette fonction est aussi dotée d'une cloche qui sonne à la fin de la durée programmée.
- **Témoin « ON »** - S'allume lorsque le four est en fonction.
- **Lèchefrite** Pour faire griller et rôtir les viandes, la volaille, le poisson et autres.

AVERTISSEMENT: AFIN DE RÉDUIRE LES RISQUES DE BLESSURE OU DE BRÛLURE, NE TOUCHEZ PAS AUX SURFACES CHAUDES LORSQUE LE FOUR EST EN FONCTION. UTILISEZ TOUJOURS DES GANTS DE CUISSON.

Mise en garde: Soyez toujours extrêmement prudent lorsque vous retirez la rôtissoire, la grille ou tout récipient chaud d'un four. Utilisez toujours des gants de cuisine lorsque vous retirez des articles chauds du four.

Les éléments chauffants supérieurs s'allument et s'éteignent afin de conserver la température maximale dans le four. Pour de meilleurs résultats, le four devrait être préchauffé à 450° F durant 20 minutes avant de mettre de la nourriture à griller.

Fonctionnement

- Réglez la température à **450° F.**
- Tournez le bouton de fonction à la position « **Broil**» (gril). Préchauffez le four.
- Placez la grille sur le plateau à miettes.
- Placez le plat sur la grille et faites-la glisser dans le porte-grille supérieur ou intermédiaire selon l'épaisseur du plat que vous préparez.
- La nourriture devrait être placée le plus près possible de l'élément chauffant supérieur, sans y toucher.
- Réglez à la température désirée.
- Badigeonnez la nourriture avec des sauces ou de l'huile, si désiré.
- Tournez la minuterie à la position « **Stay On** » (demeurer en fonction).
- Laissez la porte **légèrement entrouverte.**
- Une fois la cuisson terminée, tournez la minuterie à la position « **OFF** » **(arrêt).**

Guide de gril

Les résultats peuvent varier selon l'épaisseur des aliments grillés. Ajustez la durée de cuisson selon vos besoins. Rappelez-vous aussi de retourner la viande ou le poisson à la moitié de la cuisson et de surveiller le gril pour éviter de les brûler.

VIANDE	TEMPÉRATURE	DURÉE
BIFTECK DE CÔTE	400	20-25 min.
BIFTECK D'ALOYAU	400	20-25 min.
HAMBOURGEOIS	400	15-25 min.
CÔTELETTES DE PORC	400	25-35 min.
CÔTELETTES D'AGNEAU	400	30-40 min.
CUISSES DE POULET	400	25-35 min.
FILETS DE POISSON	350	15-25 min.
DARNES DE SAUMON	350	15-25 min.

Avertissement: Toutes les durées de cuisson sont basées sur des viandes réfrigérées. Les viandes surgelées peuvent nécessiter une durée plus longue. L'utilisation d'un thermomètre à viande est donc fortement recommandée.

Faites cuire vos biscuits, gâteaux, tartes, carrés au chocolat, etc. préférés. Les récipients pouvant entrer dans votre four sont de longueur maximale de 9 pouces. L'utilisation de sacs de cuisson ou de récipients de verre dans le four n'est pas recommandé. **N'utilisez jamais** de plastique, carton ou autre produit semblable dans le four.

Remarque: Placez la grille sur le porte-grille inférieur.

Fonctionnement

- Placez la grille sur le porte-grille **inférieur ou intermédiaire** selon la hauteur de votre plat, ou selon la recette.
- Placez le plateau avec les articles à cuire sur la grille.
- Tournez le bouton de fonction à la position « **Bake** » (cuisson). Tournez la minuterie à la position « **Stay On** »(demeurer en fonction).
- Une fois la cuisson terminée, tournez la minuterie à la position **« OFF » (arrêt).**

Position de la grille

Biscuits - Utilisez les portes grille inférieur et intermédiaire.
Gâteaux à étage - Utilisez le porte grille inférieur (faites cuire un étage à la fois).
Tartes - Utilisez le porte grille inférieur.

Cuisson des biscuits

Pour la cuisson des biscuits, nous vous suggérons de régler la température de cuisson et d'utiliser une plaque à biscuits sur la grille. En outre, l'utilisation d'un papier à cuisson sur la plaque à biscuits pourra s'avérer utile pour certains types de biscuits.

1. Utilisez un papier à cuisson sur la plaque à biscuits afin d'empêcher les biscuits de coller.
2. Les plaques à biscuits, durées de cuisson et températures peuvent varier de celles nécessaires à d'autres produits de cuisson.

Guide de cuisson

Suivez les instructions se trouvant sur l'emballage ou dans la recette pour la durée et la température de cuisson.

Tailles de plateaux de cuisson recommandées

Les tailles de plateaux de cuisson suivantes devraient convenir à votre four grille-pain. Assurez-vous que le plateau convient à votre four avant de préparer votre recette.

   plateau de 6 muffins
   plateau à pain de 8 x 4
   plateau à pain de 9 x 5
   plateau rond ou carré de 8 po
   chaudron de 1-1/2 litre – la plupart des formats.

Lorsque vous cuisinez avec des plateaux à pain, ne les remplissez pas à plus de la moitié.

Grille-pain

Le four grande capacité permet de griller de 4 à 6 tranches de pain, 6 muffins ou 6 gaufres ou crêpes surgelées. Lorsque vous ne grillez qu'un ou deux articles, placez la nourriture sur la grille, au centre du four.

Fonctionnement

- Réglez la température à 450° F.
- Tournez le bouton de fonction à la position « **Toast** » (grille-pain).
- Placez la nourriture sur la grille.
- Assurez-vous que le plateau à miettes est en place.
- Tournez la minuterie à la cuisson désirée (Light (légère) à Dark (foncée).
- La cloche signale la fin du cycle de grille-pain.

Remarque: La grille devrait être placée au centre du four, les onglets vers le bas.

Réglages de grille-pain:

Léger :   4 min.
Moyen :   7 min.
Foncé :   9 min.

MISE EN GARDE: Lorsque vous grillez des aliments, ne les laissez pas plus longtemps que les durées indiquées ci-dessus. Griller les aliments plus longtemps les brûlera.

GARANTIE LIMITÉE DE UN (1) AN

EURO-PRO Operating LLC garantit ce produit contre toute défectuosité matérielle ou de main d'œuvre pour une période de un (1) an à compter de la date d'achat, dans le cadre d'une utilisation domestique normale, en vertu des conditions, exclusions et exceptions suivantes.
Si votre appareil cesse de fonctionner correctement dans le cadre d'un usage domestique normal pendant la période de garantie, retournez-le avec ses accessoires, retour pré-affranchi, à :
É.-U. :   *EURO-PRO Operating LLC*, 94 Main Mill Street, Door 16, Plattsburgh, NY 12901
Au Canada : *EURO-PRO Operating LLC*, 4400 Bois Franc, St-Laurent (Québec) H4S 1A7
Si *EURO-PRO* constate que l'appareil comporte une défectuosité matérielle ou de main d'œuvre, *EURO-PRO* le réparera ou le remplacera sans frais de votre part. Une preuve d'achat indiquant la date d'achat et un montant de 18,95 $ pour la manutention et l'envoi de retour doivent être inclus.*
La responsabilité de *EURO-PRO Operating LLC* ne se limite qu'au coût des pièces de rechange ou de l'appareil, à notre discrétion. Cette garantie ne couvre pas l'usure normale des pièces et ne couvre pas les appareils altérés ou utilisés à des fins commerciales. Cette garantie limitée exclut les dommages causés par le mésusage, l'abus, la manipulation négligente ainsi que par une manutention en transit ou un emballage inadéquats. Cette garantie ne couvre pas les défectuosités ou dommages découlant directement ou indirectement du transport, des réparations, des altérations ou de l'entretien apportés au produit ou à ses pièces par un réparateur non autorisé par *EURO-PRO* .
Cette garantie couvre l'acheteur initial du produit et exclut toute autre garantie juridique ou conventionnelle. Le cas échéant, *EURO-PRO Operating LLC* n'est tenue qu'aux obligations spécifiques assumées par elle de façon expresse en vertu des conditions de cette garantie limitée.**En aucun cas** *EURO-PRO Operating LLC* ne sera-t-elle tenue responsable de dommages indirects de quelque nature que ce soit. Certains états ou provinces n'autorisent pas l'exclusion ou la limitation des dommages indirects. Ainsi, la disposition ci-devant pourrait ne pas s'appliquer à vous.
Cette garantie vous confère des droits juridiques précis pouvant varier d'un état ou d'une province à l'autre.

*Important : Emballez soigneusement l'appareil afin d'éviter tout dommage durant le transport. Avant d'emballer l'appareil, assurez-vous d'y apposer une étiquette portant vos nom, adresse complète et numéro de téléphone ainsi qu'une note précisant les détails de l'achat, le modèle et le problème éprouvé par l'appareil. Nous vous recommandons d'assurer votre colis (les dommages survenus durant le transport ne sont pas couverts par la garantie). Indiquez « AUX SOINS DU SERVICE À LA CLIENTÈLE » sur l'emballage extérieur. Comme nous nous efforçons en tout temps d'améliorer nos produits, les spécifications décrites dans ce guide sont sujettes à changement sans préavis.

FICHE D'ENREGISTREMENT DU PROPRIÉTAIRE
CONSOMMATEURS CANADIENS SEULEMENT

Veuillez remplir cette fiche d'enregistrement et la poster dans les dix (10) jours suivant l'achat. L'enregistrement nous permettra de communiquer avec vous en cas d'avis sur la sécurité du produit. En nous retournant cette fiche, vous convenez avoir lu et compris les consignes d'utilisation et les avertissements qui les accompagnent.

RETOURNEZ À *EURO-PRO Operating LLC*, 4400 Bois-Franc, St-Laurent (Québec) H4S 1A7

Modèles TO284/TO284L

_____
Modèle de l'appareil

_____
Date d'achat   Nom du détaillant

_____
Nom du propriétaire

_____
Adresse   Ville   Prov.   Code postal

GREEN APPLE CHUTNEY

(Chatni Kachche Sebon ki)

Serves	6
Preparation time	*10 minutes*
Cooking time	*35 minutes*

This chutney can be made in large quantities, as it lasts for several days. Normally a sweet relish, I have made it a sweet-and-sour concoction by the addition of lemon juice. Good as a side dish, and goes with packed lunches, too!

Imperial (Metric)	American
4 medium, green apples	4 medium, green apples
2 small onions	2 small onions
2 cloves garlic	2 cloves garlic
½ teaspoon grated ginger root	½ teaspoon grated ginger root
Water as needed	Water as needed
1 tablespoon lemon juice	1 tablespoon lemon juice
4 oz (100g) raw cane sugar	½ cup raw sugar
Sea salt to taste	Sea salt to taste
Pinch of red chilli powder	Dash of red chili powder
½ pint (300ml) cider vinegar	1¼ cups cider vinegar
1 teaspoon sultanas	1 teaspoon golden raisins

1

Wash, dry, and peel the apples, onions, garlic, and ginger; core the apples, and chop all the ingredients finely.

2

Place them in a saucepan; add a little water, and bring to a boil. Stir in the lemon juice and sugar, and continue to cook over moderate heat another 5 minutes.

3

Add the rest of the ingredients, lower the heat, and go on cooking until the chutney assumes a thick and smooth consistency — about 15 to 20 minutes.

4

Remove pan from heat, and store the chutney in a suitable covered container while still warm.

5

Serve when needed.

RHUBARB CHUTNEY

(Rewatcheeni Chatni)

Serves 10 helpings or more	
Preparation time 10 minutes	
Cooking time 25 minutes	

This is another tasty example of culinary chemistry; most of the ingredients in this recipe are freely used in western kitchens and yet it produces a typically eastern flavour! Serve as a side dish with an Indian or western meal. Make a larger quantity if you wish, as this chutney lasts for a few days.

Imperial (Metric)	*American*
½ lb (225g) rhubarb, ready weight	½ pound rhubarb, ready weight
1 pint (600ml) water	2½ cups water
4 oz (100g) jaggery (unrefined palm sugar)	¼ cup jaggery (unrefined palm sugar)
Small pinch of asafoetida powder	Small dash of asafoetida powder
1 teaspoon garam masala	1 teaspoon garam masala
½ teaspoon nigella (kalaunji)	½ teaspoon nigella (kalaunji)
1 clove garlic, sliced	1 clove garlic, sliced
½ teaspoon grated ginger root	½ teaspoon grated ginger root
Pinch of sea salt	Dash of sea salt
½ teaspoon red chilli powder	½ teaspoon red chili powder
3 tablespoons lemon juice	¼ cup lemon juice

1

Wash, peel, and cut the rhubarb in small pieces so as to get the ready weight.

2

Place the rhubarb, water, and jaggery in a saucepan, and put over medium heat. Cook, stirring, about 5 to 7 minutes.

3

Add the next 5 ingredients — from asafoetida to ginger root — and cook, stirring, another 5 minutes.

4

Stir in the salt and chilli powder, and cook 5 more minutes. Then add the lemon juice, cover pan, lower heat, and simmer another 10 minutes.

5

Remove pan from heat, and let cool; serve as needed. Left-overs can go into the refrigerator or in a lidded container for later use.

POTATO CHUTNEY

(Aalu Chatni)

| Serves 4 |
| Preparation time   10 minutes |
| Cooking time   25 minutes |

This must be the most extraordinary use ever of the potato; but the concoction has the eastern promise and delightful taste. Do adjust the quantity to be served per person, and the quantity of chutney to be made in one batch; it can last a few days.

Imperial (Metric)	American
4 medium potatoes	4 medium potatoes
2 oz (50g) raw cane sugar	¼ cup raw sugar
1 pint (600ml) water	2½ cups water
1 teaspoon sliced ginger root	1 teaspoon sliced ginger root
1 tablespoon chopped onion	1 tablespoon chopped onion
1 teaspoon sultanas	1 teaspoon golden raisins
1 teaspoon pistachios, sliced (or another nut of your choice)	1 teaspoon pistachios, sliced (or another nut of your choice)
4 tablespoons cider vinegar	⅓ cup cider vinegar
Sea salt to taste	Sea salt to taste
½ teaspoon red chilli powder	½ teaspoon red chili powder

1

Wash potatoes, and scrape off the outer skins; then quarter them.

2

Place the potatoes, together with sugar and measured water, in a deep saucepan, and bring to a boil over moderate heat.

3

Grind the ginger and onion together, and add to the boiling mixture; add the dried fruit and nuts and cook another 5 minutes or so.

4

Stir in the vinegar, salt, and chilli powder; lower heat, and cook another 10 minutes.

5

Serve when cool; any left-overs can be stored in the refrigerator or in a lidded jar.

DRIED PLUM CHUTNEY

(Aalu Buckhaare ki Chatni)

Serves	10 helpings or more
Preparation time	15 minutes plus soaking time
Cooking time	30 minutes

This marvellous chutney is often served with a formal meal on special occasions. It can be on the expensive side and should not be kept for more than 2 days. However, feel free to make it when the mood strikes you, and it should taste splendid every time!

Imperial (Metric)	American
½ lb (225g) dried plums	½ pound dried plums
4 dried dates	4 dried dates
1 tablespoon sultanas	1 tablespoon golden raisins
4 oz (100g) raw cane sugar	½ cup raw sugar
1 tablespoon nuts of your choice (pistachios, cashews, and walnuts), shredded	1 tablespoon nuts of your choice (pistachios, cashews, and walnuts), shredded
½ teaspoon each of coriander, fenugreek, mustard and white cumin seeds, and fennel, dry roasted and coarsely ground together	½ teaspoon each of coriander, fenugreek, mustard and white cumin seeds, and fennel, dry roasted and coarsely ground together
½ teaspoon grated, fresh ginger	½ teaspoon grated, fresh ginger
Sea salt to taste	Sea salt to taste
1 teaspoon cayenne	1 teaspoon cayenne
6 tablespoons lemon juice	½ cup lemon juice
Pinch of crushed saffron strands	Dash of crushed saffron strands

1

Soak the dried plums in 1 pint (600ml/2½ cups) water about 4 hours; separately clean and soak the dried dates and sultanas (golden raisins) in water, too.

2

Boil the plums in the water used for soaking; remove the pan from the heat, separate and discard the pits from the plums, and mash the flesh into the water. Add the sugar, return to heat, and cook another 10 minutes over moderate heat.

3

Remove the dates (separating and discarding the stones) and sultanas (raisins) from the water and chop. Add these, together with the nuts, to the cooking mixture and stir well.

4

Stir in the spices, ginger, salt, cayenne, and lemon juice, and bring the mixture to a boil. Add the saffron, cover the pan, and remove it from the heat to cool — about 10 minutes.

5

Serve as needed. Store the remainder in a covered container or in the refrigerator for later use.

BANANA CHUTNEY

(Kela Chatni)

Serves 4
Preparation time   10 minutes plus chilling time

This concoction uses mostly western ingredients and produces an occidental taste! Instead of going into theories, I suggest you make this chutney and find out for yourself. A delightful side dish, usually served chilled.

Imperial (Metric)	*American*
1 large banana	1 large banana
2 tablespoons desiccated coconut	2 tablespoons dried coconut
A pinch each of black cumin and mustard seeds, roasted and ground	A dash each of black cumin and mustard seeds, roasted and ground
Sea salt to taste	Sea salt to taste
1 small green chilli, ground	1 small green chili, ground
Pinch of green cardamom powder	Dash of green cardamom powder
2 tablespoons lemon juice	2 tablespoons lemon juice
1 tablespoon finely shredded mint leaves	1 tablespoon finely shredded mint leaves

1

Peel the banana and mash it up; then place it in an electric blender (or use a hand whisk).

2

Add the rest of the ingredients, except the mint, in the order of listing, and blend thoroughly.

3

Remove to a serving dish. Garnish with mint leaves.

4

Refrigerate before serving.

KHOYA CHUTNEY

(Chatni khoye ki)

Serves 4
Preparation time   10 minutes
Cooking time   25 minutes

If you were looking for a most unusual chutney even from an Indian standpoint, your search is over, this is it. Either buy ready-made khoya from your Indian grocer, or make it at home (see page 24), and delight your guests either way.

Imperial (Metric)	American
4 oz (100g) khoya	¼ pound khoya
2 tablespoons ghee	2 tablespoons ghee
1 teaspoon each of white cumin seeds and mustard seeds, dry roasted and ground	1 teaspoon each of white cumin seeds and mustard seeds, dry roasted and ground
Pinch of green cardamom powder	Dash of green cardamom powder
2 tablespoons tamarind juice	2 tablespoons tamarind juice
2 oz (50g) raw cane sugar	¼ cup raw sugar
1 oz (25g) mixture of chopped almonds, pistachios, and sultanas	3 tablespoons mixed chopped almonds, pistachios, and golden raisins
Pinch of crushed saffron sprigs	Dash of crushed saffron sprigs
2 tablespoons lemon juice	2 tablespoons lemon juice
Sea salt to taste	Sea salt to taste

1

Break up the khoya into small pieces. Heat half the ghee in a saucepan, add the khoya, and stir-fry until golden — about 5 minutes. Remove pan from heat, and let cool.

2

Heat the remaining ghee in another saucepan, and sauté the cumin, mustard, and cardamom powder over moderate heat about 2 minutes. Add the tamarind juice and sugar, and bring to a bubbling boil.

3

Keeping the saucepan on the heat, add the khoya, nuts, and sultanas (raisins) as well as saffron and lemon juice; blend well, cover the pan, and cook for another 10 minutes.

4

Sprinkle in the salt, stir the mixture, and remove pan from heat; let cool. Serve as needed.

PAPAYA CHUTNEY

(Papeeta Chatni)

Serves	*4*
Preparation time	*10 minutes*
Cooking time	*30 minutes*

A very nice chutney, if a little unusual and requiring an acquired taste. Like other chutneys, this one offers some scope for experimentation. Once you are initiated, this will prove to be a pleasant side dish with a meal or with savoury snacks.

Imperial (Metric)	American
½ lb (225g) papaya	½ pound papaya
1 teaspoon sliced ginger root	1 teaspoon sliced ginger root
2 cloves garlic, sliced	2 cloves garlic, sliced
1 tablespoon chopped onion	1 tablespoon chopped onion
½ pint (300ml) water	1¼ cups water
½ lb (225g) jaggery	1 cup jaggery
Sea salt to taste	Sea salt to taste
1 teaspoon red chilli powder	1 teaspoon red chili powder
4 tablespoons tamarind juice	⅓ cup tamarind juice
1 heaped teaspoon garam masala	1 heaped teaspoon garam masala

1
Wash and peel the papaya; cut into slices.

2
Place the papaya in a saucepan, together with ginger root, garlic, onion, and the measured water, and bring to a boil over moderate heat.

3
Add the jaggery to the cooking mixture. Add the salt and chilli powder, and continue to cook another 5 minutes.

4
Stir in the tamarind juice and garam masala, and mix thoroughly; cook another 10 minutes, or until the chutney thickens to the desired consistency.

5
Remove pan from heat, and let cool; serve as needed. Any leftovers can go into the refrigerator to be served at the next meal.

PINEAPPLE CHUTNEY

(Anannaas Chatni)

Serves	4
Preparation time	10 minutes
Cooking time	25 minutes

It may come as a surprise to western readers, but a truly delicious and mysteriously exotic relish can be prepared with pineapple. Serve it with western dishes, too.

Imperial (Metric)	American
½ lb (225g) pineapple flesh, chopped	1 cup pineapple flesh, chopped
Water as needed	Water as needed
½ teaspoon each of mustard and turmeric powders	½ teaspoon each of mustard and turmeric powders
1 tablespoon raw cane sugar	1 tablespoon raw sugar
1 tablespoon sultanas	1 tablespoon golden raisins
Sea salt to taste (1 teaspoon)	Sea salt to taste (1 teaspoon)
3 tablespoons lemon juice	¼ cup lemon juice
A pinch each of cardamom and red chilli powders	A dash each of cardamom and red chili powders

1

Place the pineapple in a saucepan, add enough water to cover the pieces, and bring to a boil. Remove pan from heat, and drain off the water.

2

Sprinkle the mustard and turmeric powders over the pineapple pieces, and mix thoroughly. Place the spiced pineapple in a saucepan, and put over moderate heat. Cook, stirring, about 2 minutes.

3

Add ½ pint (300ml/1¼ cups) water together with sugar, sultanas (raisins), salt, and lemon juice; lower heat, cover pan, and bring to a boil — about 10 to 15 minutes.

4

Take off the lid, and sprinkle the cardamom and chilli powders over the preparation; put the lid back on, remove the saucepan from the heat, and let cool slowly — about 10 to 15 minutes.

5

Serve when cool; left-overs can go into the refrigerator or a covered container for subsequent use.

DRIED FRUIT AND NUT CHUTNEY

(Sukhe Mevon ki Chatni)

Serves	6
Preparation time	15 minutes
Cooking time	25 minutes

This is a novel sweet chutney. You can also make it with water and lemon juice. There is plenty of opportunity to substitute dried fruits and nuts of your choice. A stylish and muscular side dish!

Imperial (Metric)	American
½ lb (225g) mixed nuts and dried fruit (e.g. walnuts, cashews, sultanas, and dates)	2 cups mixed nuts and dried fruit (e.g. walnuts, cashews, golden raisins, and dates)
1 teaspoon each of coriander seeds, fennel, and nigella	1 teaspoon each of coriander seeds, fennel, and nigella
1 teaspoon raw cane sugar	1 teaspoon raw sugar
Sea salt to taste	Sea salt to taste
½ teaspoon red chilli powder	½ teaspoon red chili powder
½ pint (300ml) cider vinegar	1¼ cups cider vinegar

1
Clean the nuts and dried fruit, and then chop.

2
Place in a saucepan; add some water, and bring to a boil. Add the spices (either whole or crushed, according to choice) and cook another 2 minutes.

3
Put the rest of the ingredients into the pan, and simmer over moderate heat about 10 minutes. This chutney should not get too thick.

4
Remove pan from heat, and let cool.

5
Serve as needed; store the left-overs in a jar for later use.

Chapter 3

Sauces
(Raseeli Chatniyaan)

Most Indian meals are accompanied by a chutney or sauce of some kind; they enhance the taste of a meal and lend it colour. Sauces, like chutneys, titillate the taste buds and give a fillip to the flow of digestive juices. They can be hot and pungent, or they can be mild and gentle; thus, they suit all palates.

Sauces are much thinner in consistency than are chutneys, and they entail a rather elaborate preparation. They are made in various ways from sugar, vinegar, milk, or water, together with fruits and vegetables. Any condiments and spices to be used are usually added towards the end of the sauce's creation. Some sauces, such as saambhar and cumin are served with specific dishes. In general, however, sauces are served as toppings for various savoury dishes. They add variety to taste.

When the sauce is ready, it should be stored in a clean, dry, sterilized, and airtight container of a suitable size; the container should be covered tightly after each use to keep it fresh and last longer. Keep the container in a cool place.

SAAMBHAR SAUCE

(Saambhar Paani)

Serves	*4*
Preparation time	*20 minutes plus soaking time*
Cooking time	*1 hour*

This sauce is the inevitable companion of many South Indian dishes and plain rice preparations. Use seasonal vegetables of your choice for this sauce, in addition to standard vegetables like the potato and cauliflower. The amount of water can be adjusted according to personal preference.

Imperial (Metric)	American
2 tablespoons brown grams	2 tablespoons brown grams
Water as needed	Water as needed
½ lb (225g) mixture of toor and urad daals	1 cup mixture of toor and urad daals
Sea salt as needed	Sea salt as needed
Pinch of turmeric powder	Dash of turmeric powder
1 tablespoon mustard oil	1 tablespoon mustard oil
Pinch of asafoetida powder	Dash of asafoetida powder
1 green chilli, chopped	1 green chili, chopped
1 tablespoon grated onion	1 tablespoon grated onion
1 tablespoon saambhar powder	1 tablespoon saambhar powder
½ lb (225g) mixed vegetables, convenient pieces	1½ cups mixed vegetables, convenient pieces
1 tablespoon desiccated coconut	1 tablespoon dried coconut
1 tablespoon lemon juice	1 tablespoon lemon juice
1 tablespoon green coriander, chopped	1 tablespoon green cilantro, chopped

1

Soak the brown grams in water to cover for at least 4 hours; then drain off the water and coarsely grind them.

2

Place the daal mixture in a deep saucepan, add 2½ cups water together with 1 teaspoon sea salt and the turmeric, and boil 30 to 40 minutes, or until the daal is tender; keep stirring so that the mixture does not stick to the bottom of the pan. Keep the heat at moderate.

3

Heat the oil in a frying pan, and cook asafoetida, chilli, and onion until deep golden. Stir in the saambhar powder, and cook another minute. Now add the ground chick peas (garbanzo beans), and cook 5 minutes, stirring.

4

Add the frying mixture to the cooking daal, pour in another 1 pint (600ml/2½ cups) water together with additional salt to taste, add the vegetables, and cook over medium heat 10 to 15 minutes, or until the vegetables are tender.

5

Add the coconut and lemon juice, blend well, and remove pan from heat. Garnish with green coriander (cilantro), and serve piping hot.

VINEGAR SAUCE

(Sirka Chat Pata)

Serves	10 helpings or more
Preparation time	15 minutes plus maturing time

This is an interesting concoction that offers a tremendous scope for experimentation with alternatives. Some people prefer to serve it as soon as it is prepared; I suggest you wait as instructed for a better taste.

Imperial (Metric)	American
2 oz (50g) mint leaves	2 ounces mint leaves
8 cloves garlic, whole	8 cloves garlic, whole
8 button onions, whole	8 button onions, whole
8 dried, red chillies, whole	8 dried, red chilies, whole
1 pint (600ml) cider vinegar	2½ cups cider vinegar
1 teaspoon sea salt, or to taste	1 teaspoon sea salt, or to taste
1 teaspoon raw cane sugar (optional)	1 teaspoon raw sugar (optional)

1

Wash and dry the mint leaves. Wash and peel the garlic and onions. Wipe the chillies, and remove their top stalks, if any.

2

Place the ingredients, as prepared in step 1, in a lidded glass jar; pour the vinegar into the jar, and add the salt and sugar. Blend carefully but thoroughly.

3

Cover the jar opening. Traditionally, a piece of clean muslin cloth is placed on the mouth of the jar before the lid is tightly placed into position.

4

Put the jar out in the sun for about a week, or until the garlic and onion are the same colour as vinegar. In the absence of hot sun, keep the jar in the warmest place in the house, but for a total of about two weeks.

5

Serve when needed, replacing the lid tightly after each use.

MANGO SAUCE

(Aam ka Ras)

Serves   4

Preparation time   20 minutes plus chilling time

Cooking time   15 minutes

This is a magical dish which serves as a drink in itself, and also as a sauce to add variety to the taste of a dish; adjust the amount of water and the condiments. As a drink it cools you down in the summer and tastes sweet-and-sour; as a sauce, it tastes out of this world!

Imperial (Metric)	American
4 green mangoes	4 green mangoes
Water as needed	Water as needed
1 tablespoon raw cane sugar	1 tablespoon raw sugar
1 teaspoon sea salt, or to taste	1 teaspoon sea salt, or to taste
Large pinch of cayenne	Large dash of cayenne
2 oz (50g) fresh mint, ground	2 ounces fresh mint, ground
½ teaspoon white cumin seeds, roasted and ground	½ teaspoon white cumin seeds, roasted and ground
Crushed ice, to serve	Crushed ice, to serve

1

Boil the mangoes in water to cover for about 10 minutes; then drain off the water and peel, stone, and pulp the mangoes in a deep bowl.

2

Add the sugar and 1 pint (600ml/2½ cups) water to the mango pulp, and whisk thoroughly (for sauce use only ½ or ¼ of the prescribed water).

3

Stir in the salt, cayenne, and ground mint and whisk again. Add the ground cumin and blend well.

4

Pour into tall glasses, and serve topped with crushed ice (as a sauce, just chill and serve; there is no need to add ice).

TOMATO SAUCE

(Tamaatar-Sirka)

Serves	16 helpings or more
Preparation time	15 minutes
Cooking time	25 minutes

This is an exotic Oriental sauce and nothing like its bottled cousin sold in western supermarkets! Like many other Indian dishes, this one also lends itself to experimentation with alternatives of your choice. It is handy to have around the house; serve with savoury snacks.

Imperial (Metric)	American
2 lb (900g) ripe tomatoes	2 pounds ripe tomatoes
1 lb (450g) raw cane sugar	2 cups raw sugar
4 oz (100g) garlic cloves	4 ounces garlic cloves
4 oz (100g) fresh ginger	4 ounces green ginger
2 teaspoons sultanas	2 teaspoons golden raisins
½ pint (300ml) cider vinegar	1¼ cups cider vinegar
Sea salt to taste	Sea salt to taste
1 teaspoon red chilli powder	1 teaspoon red chili powder
Pinch of garam masala	Dash of garam masala

1

Steam the tomatoes; then skin and mash them in a large saucepan. Add the sugar, and put the pan over medium heat; keep cooking and stirring until well blended — about 5 minutes.

2

Clean and chop the garlic, ginger, and sultanas (raisins), and add to the cooking mixture.

3

Pour in the vinegar together with the remaining ingredients, and stir thoroughly. Keep cooking until the mixture thickens to the desired consistency — about 15 minutes.

4

Remove the pan from the heat, and store the sauce in an airtight container; keep in a cool place.

5

Serve when needed, covering the container after each use.

CUMIN SAUCE

(Zeera Paani)

Serves 6

Preparation time 15 minutes plus soaking and chilling time

This sauce is usually served with the chaat dish "golgappa", but it can also be served by itself as an appetizing drink (in that case, add crushed ice to each serving). This popular sauce has been made in many parts of India since ancient times. It is made from many recipes, and this is one of the better ones!

Imperial (Metric)	*American*
4 oz (100g) seedless tamarind pulp	¼ pound seedless tamarind pulp
1 pint (600ml) warm water	2½ cups warm water
1 green chilli	1 green chili
1 oz (25g) green mint	1 ounce green mint
¼ teaspoon grated, fresh ginger	¼ teaspoon grated, fresh ginger
Sea salt to taste	Sea salt to taste
Pinch of black salt	Dash of black salt
½ teaspoon red chilli powder	½ teaspoon red chili powder
½ teaspoon white cumin seeds, roasted and ground	½ teaspoon white cumin seeds, roasted and ground
1 teaspoon garam masala	1 teaspoon garam masala
1 tablespoon fresh lemon juice	1 tablespoon fresh lemon juice

1

Soak the tamarind in warm water about 20 minutes, then mash it thoroughly. Push the liquid through a muslin cloth (or a sieve) into a bowl, and discard the remaining husk.

2

Grind the chilli, mint, and ginger together with the salt, and add to the strained liquid; stir and mix completely.

3

Add the red chilli powder, ground cumin and garam masala and whisk briskly for a few seconds.

4

Mix in lemon juice; chill and serve.

MILK SAUCE

(Doodh Masala)

Serves   10 helpings or more
Preparation time   10 minutes
Cooking time   30 minutes

This concoction also regales in the name of white sauce; you may serve it hot or cold. Adjust the hotness and consistency to your liking.

Imperial (Metric)	American
1 medium onion	1 medium onion
1 large carrot	1 large carrot
4 oz (100g) butter	½ cup butter
1 tablespoon grated cheese	1 tablespoon grated cheese
3 tablespoons wholemeal flour	¼ cup whole wheat flour
1 pint (600ml) milk	2½ cups milk
Sea salt to taste	Sea salt to taste
Pinch of ground black pepper	Dash of ground black pepper
½ teaspoon ground mustard seeds	½ teaspoon ground mustard seeds

1

Clean, dry, and grate the onion and carrot separately.

2

Heat the butter in a deep saucepan; add the onion and stir until golden. Then stir in the carrot and cheese; cook over moderate heat until well blended.

3

Add the flour and cook, stirring, until the flour is golden and gives out a pleasant aroma.

4

Pour in the milk together with the remaining ingredients, one by one; lower heat and cook 15 to 20 minutes, or until the sauce assumes the desired consistency. Make sure the milk does not boil.

5

Serve hot, or store in an airtight container to serve cold later.

APPLE-PINEAPPLE SAUCE

(Seb-Anannas Paani)

Serves	*10 helpings or more*
Preparation time	*20 minutes*
Cooking time	*25 minutes*

This is a delightful sauce, which with a thicker consistency can be served with savoury snacks or as a side dish with a main meal. Make it thinner and it could become a very likaeble drink by itself! It is usually served cold.

Imperial (Metric)	*American*
2 sweet apples	2 sweet apples
½ lb (225g) pineapple flesh, chopped	1 cup pineapple flesh, chopped
1 pint (600ml) water	2½ cups water
2 tablespoons raw cane sugar	2 tablespoons raw sugar
½ teaspoon sea salt	½ teaspoon sea salt
4 cloves, ground	4 cloves, ground
Pinch of green cardamom powder	Dash of green cardamom powder
Pinch of crushed saffron strands	Dash of crushed saffron strands

1
Peel, core, and chop the apples.

2
Place the apple and pineapple in a saucepan. Add water and cook over moderate heat until the apple is tender — about 10 minutes.

3
Remove pan from heat, and mash contents together; push through a sieve into another saucepan and return to heat.

4
Stir in the rest of the ingredients, saffron last, and cook until the sauce is of the desired consistency — another 10 minutes or so.

5
Store in a dry glass jar or bottle, and serve as needed. Cover the container after each use.

GINGER-MANGO SAUCE

(Sonth-Amchoor)

Serves	*10 helpings or more*
Preparation time	*15 minutes plus soaking time*
Cooking time	*35 minutes*

This sweet-and-sour sauce is often served on its own as a side dish with a main meal; it can also be served as a topping on yogurt-based savouries and chaat dishes. A good vehicle for producing colour contrasts on the dining table!

Imperial (Metric)	*American*
2 tablespoons sultanas	2 tablespoons golden raisins
2 tablespoons chopped dry dates	2 tablespoons chopped dried dates
1 tablespoon sliced fresh ginger	1 tablespoon sliced green ginger
4 oz (100g) dried green mango slices (amchoor)	¼ pound dried green mango slices (amchoor)
1 pint (600ml) water	2½ cups water
½ lb (225g) molasses (gur)	1½ cups molasses (gur)
Sea salt to taste	Sea salt to taste
½ teaspoon coarsely ground coriander seeds	½ teaspoon coarsely ground coriander seeds
Pinch of garam masala	Dash of garam masala
1 teaspoon cayenne	1 teaspoon cayenne
Chopped green coriander, to serve (optional)	Chopped cilantro, to serve (optional)

1

Soak the sultanas (raisins), dates, and ginger in water to cover about 1 hour.

2

Place the mango, measured water, and molasses in a deep saucepan, and bring to a boil; go on cooking over moderate heat until the mango slices are tender.

3

Remove pan from heat; mash the contents together and push through a fine sieve. Transfer the liquid to the saucepan, and return to heat.

4

Drain the sultanas (raisins), dates, and ginger, and add to the cooking liquid. Stir in the salt, coriander (cilantro), garam masala, and the cayenne, and blend thoroughly. Cover the pan, and continue to cook over medium heat for another 15 to 20 minutes.

5

Remove pan from heat. When cool, put the sauce in a jar or bottle and store in the refrigerator.

6

Serve when needed and sprinkle with the green coriander if desired.

ONION SAUCE

(Pyaazi Saas)

Serves 8 helpings or more	
Preparation time 10 minutes	
Cooking time 25 minutes	

This is an exotic sauce for hot-blooded people! You may serve it hot or cold; either way it is sure to inject fresh life into the blandest meal.

Imperial (Metric)	*American*
2 oz (50g) ghee	¼ cup ghee
2 medium onions, finely chopped	2 medium onions, finely chopped
4 cloves garlic, chopped	4 cloves garlic, chopped
1 tablespoon wholemeal flour	1 tablespoon whole wheat flour
½ pint (300ml) cider vinegar	1¼ cups cider vinegar
1 teaspoon raw cane sugar	1 teaspoon raw sugar
Sea salt to taste	Sea salt to taste
Seeds of 1 brown cardamom	Seeds of 1 brown cardamom
8 black peppercorns, whole	8 black peppercorns, whole
Pinch of cayenne	Dash of cayenne

1

Heat the ghee in a deep saucepan, and sauté the onion and garlic until light golden.

2

Add the flour and cook, stirring, until flour is golden.

3

Now pour in the vinegar and add the rest of the ingredients — one by one — and cook, covered, over medium heat until the sauce thickens — about 15 minutes.

4

Remove pan from heat, and serve the sauce hot, or store in a suitable dry and sterilized container to serve cold later.

APRICOT-PEACH SAUCE

(Khubaani-Aadu Sirka)

Serves 10 helpings or more
Preparation time 10 minutes
Cooking time 30 minutes

This is a rather classy sauce with a consistency that can be adapted to one's liking. Serve as a side dish with a main meal; it should prove popular with connoisseurs and novices alike!

Imperial (Metric)	American
½ lb (225g) apricots	4 to 6 apricots
½ lb (225g) peaches	2 peaches
1 tablespoon sultanas	1 tablespoon golden raisins
4 ripe tomatoes	4 ripe tomatoes
½ lb (225g) raw cane sugar	1 cup raw sugar
1 pint (600ml) cider vinegar	2½ cups cider vinegar
Sea salt to taste	Sea salt to taste
½ teaspoon red chilli powder	½ teaspoon red chili powder
6 cloves garlic, chopped	6 cloves garlic, chopped
2 oz (50g) grated fresh ginger	2 ounces grated fresh ginger
Small pinch each of powdered cloves, nutmeg and cinnamon	Small dash each of powdered cloves, nutmeg, and cinnamon

1

Wash and dry the apricots and peaches; then pit and chop. Clean, dry, and chop the raisins, too.

2

Place these in a deep saucepan. Chop the tomatoes and add to the pan with the sugar.

3

Cook over medium heat until they are all well blended. Mash the contents, and stir to get a smooth consistency; then push the liquid through a sieve or a piece of muslin.

4

Place the liquid in a saucepan and return to heat. Add the vinegar and the rest of the ingredients — one by one — and cook over moderate heat, stirring, until the sauce is of the needed consistency, or about 15 minutes.

5

Serve hot, or store in a sterilized container to serve cold later.

Chapter 4

Raita Dishes
(Raitay)

Yogurt is a nutritious dairy product that is the purest, most natural, and cheapest health food money can buy. Rich in calcium, protein, and iron, it is a safe vehicle to use to reduce your cholesterol intake. Yogurt also possesses healing attributes and prolongs life. Beauticians produce beauty preparations from it, and with its aid your complexion is purified and improved.

For thousands of years yogurt has enjoyed versatility and freedom in Indian cuisine. It is omnipresent not only in Indian meals, but it also figures prominently on the menus of many other cuisines of the world. Apart from being instrumental in making legendary curries and delicious drinks, yogurt is also used for marinating. However, yogurt's most notable contribution is witnessed in the raita dish. Raitas are delicious, but easy to make, yogurt dishes. They are usually served as a side dish with a main meal. These dishes boast of boosting your appetite and aiding digestion; they are very popular throughout India.

Raitas are made by mixing the yogurt with a vegetable, herb, or fruit of your choice — dried fruits and nuts, too — with different seasonings. The main ingredient has to be prepared first. Then the yogurt is beaten to a smooth consistency (add water if the mixture is too thick for your liking). The chosen seasonings are then added. As the grand finale, the raita is garnished in the age-old tradition, which does nothing but make the dish more alluring!

The west-coast dwellers of India believe that the word "raita" is derived from "rai" (mustard seeds), and they therefore make liberal use of mustard seeds in their raita preparations. In other parts of India "raita" is supposed to be "ta" (abbreviation of "taat", meaning hot). The people in these parts garnish their raitas with chilli powder. Most people chill their raitas before serving; some sauté it in hot ghee, red chilli, and mustard. Yet others make sizzling hot phuloris and then dip them into cold yogurt to make their raita!

An infinite variety of raitas is possible by using different main ingredients, combinations, and seasonings, and thereby producing a kaleidoscope of flavours! There is tremendous scope for experimentation here, depending on how adventurous you are. A raita dish usually balances a meal by serving as an antidote, to and therefore complementing, the accompanying hot and spicy dishes. I have attempted to offer in this book a collection of raitas — representative of all the various modes of raita making — made with the usual and unusual main ingredients. I hope you will like my choice.

POTATO RAITA

(Aalu Raita)

Serves 6

Preparation time   10 minutes plus chilling time

Cooking time   10 minutes

A super side dish that is ideal with a meal for the hearty eater! A very suitable offering at picnic or party time, served with an Indian bread or a rice dish.

Imperial (Metric)	American
6 medium potatoes	6 medium potatoes
1 firm, red tomato	1 firm, red tomato
½ pint (300ml) natural yogurt	1¼ cups plain yogurt
Sea salt to taste	Sea salt to taste
1 fresh green chilli, chopped	1 fresh green chili, chopped
½ teaspoon mustard seeds, ground	½ teaspoon mustard seeds, ground
1 teaspoon white cumin seeds, roasted and ground	1 teaspoon white cumin seeds, roasted and ground
1 teaspoon cayenne	1 teaspoon cayenne
1 tablespoon green coriander, finely chopped	1 tablespoon cilantro, finely chopped

1
Boil the potatoes; then peel and chop finely.

2
Finely chop the tomato; mix with the potato, and put on a plate.

3
Beat the yogurt to a smooth consistency; add the salt, green chili, and ground mustard, and beat again.

4
Add the potato-tomato mixture to the yogurt; stir in the ground cumin and blend thoroughly.

5
Garnish the raita with cayenne, and sprinkle with the coriander (cilantro).

6
Chill and serve.

ONION-TOMATO RAITA

(Pyaaz-Tamaatar Raita)

Serves 6

Preparation time 20 minutes plus chilling time

As far as possible, use spring onions (scallions) for this dish; adding tomatoes will give a fine texture to the dish. If the consistency is too thick, add a little water, and then serve chilled.

Imperial (Metric)	American
6 small spring onions	6 small scallions
(or 3 ordinary onions, medium)	(or 3 ordinary onions, medium)
3 small red and firm tomatoes	3 small red and firm tomatoes
3 small cartons natural yogurt	3 small cartons plain yogurt
Pinch of asafoetida powder	Dash of asafoetida powder
Sea salt to taste	Sea salt to taste
1 fresh green chilli, finely chopped	1 fresh green chili, finely chopped
Pinch of ground black pepper	Dash of ground black pepper
1 teaspoon white cumin seeds, roasted	1 teaspoon white cumin seeds, roasted
and ground	and ground
1 tablespoon finely chopped fresh mint	1 tablespoon finely chopped fresh mint

1
Wash and dry the onions and tomatoes, and chop finely.

2
Beat the yogurt until it assumes a smooth consistency; add asafoetida, salt, chilli, and black pepper, and beat again.

3
Stir the onion and tomato into the yogurt, and blend thoroughly.

4
Sprinkle the ground cumin over the mixture, garnish with mint, and refrigerate.

5
Serve when needed, straight from the refrigerator.

RADISH RAITA

(Mooli Raita)

Serves   6

Preparation time   20 minutes plus chilling time

This colourful concoction can be made with the white radish of the Indian variety, as well as the red radish. Its cooling and crunchy taste will easily titillate your taste buds. Serve as a side dish with a main meal.

Imperial (Metric)	American
1 lb (450g) white radish	1 pound white radish
Water as needed	Water as needed
1 pint (600ml) natural yogurt	2½ cups plain yogurt
Sea salt to taste	Sea salt to taste
Pinch of ground black pepper	Dash of ground black pepper
Pinch of cumin powder	Dash of cumin powder
½ teaspoon cayenne	½ teaspoon cayenne
1 tablespoon fresh mint, shredded	1 tablespoon fresh mint, shredded

1

Clean and wash the radish and scrape off the outer skin (leave the outer skin alone if using red radish). Grate the radish and soak in water to cover.

2

Whisk the yogurt in a deep bowl until it assumes a smooth consistency. Stir in the salt, pepper, and cumin, and whisk again.

3

Squeeze water from the radish and add to the yogurt mixture; blend thoroughly.

4

Garnish with cayenne and mint. Serve chilled.

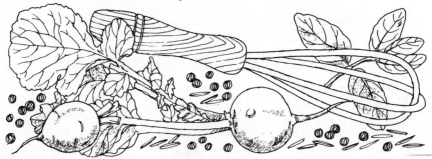

CABBAGE RAITA

(Bundgobhi Raita)

Serves   6

Preparation time   15 minutes plus chilling time

The exotic appeal of this dish is beyond comparison. It delights both ordinary and extraordinary people. When ready, this preparation should be crisp and cooling.

Imperial (Metric)	American
½ lb (225g) white cabbage	½ pound white cabbage
3 small cartons natural yogurt	3 small cartons plain yogurt
Sea salt to taste	Sea salt to taste
Pinch of garam masala	Dash of garam masala
1 tablespoon fresh mint, shredded	1 tablespoon fresh mint, shredded
½ teaspoon mustard powder	½ teaspoon mustard powder
½ teaspoon red chilli powder	½ teaspoon red chili powder

1
Wash and dry the cabbage; then shred finely.

2
Beat the yogurt and salt to a smooth consistency; add garam masala and mint, and beat again.

3
Toss in the cabbage, and blend thoroughly.

4
Garnish with mustard and chilli powders; chill and serve.

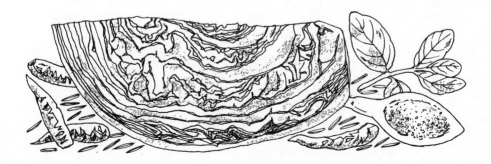

BRINJAL RAITA

(Baigan Raita)

Serves 4
Preparation time 10 minutes plus chilling time
Cooking time 10 minutes

The long aubergines (eggplants) are also called "brinjals" in India, but the normally available variety will also do. This delectable side dish is somewhat unusual although not unknown; feel free, however, to substitute any other comparable vegetable of your choice.

Imperial (Metric)	American
1 long aubergine (brinjal)	1 long eggplant
1 tablespoon ghee	1 tablespoon ghee
Sea salt as needed	Sea salt as needed
1 teaspoon cayenne	1 teaspoon cayenne
½ pint (300ml) natural yogurt	1¼ cups plain yogurt
Pinch of mustard powder	Dash of mustard powder
1 teaspoon white cumin seeds, roasted and ground	1 teaspoon white cumin seeds, roasted and ground
1 tablespoon shredded fresh mint	1 tablespoon shredded fresh mint

1
Wash the aubergine (eggplant), then slice it into long strips.

2
Heat the ghee in a frying pan. Add the aubergine (eggplant), together with a pinch of salt and half the cayenne, and cook over low heat for 5 to 7 minutes. Then remove the "red" aubergine (eggplant), and set aside.

3
Whisk the yogurt, salt to taste, the remaining cayenne, and mustard powder to a smooth consistency. Add the aubergine (eggplant), and blend thoroughly.

4
Garnish with ground cumin and mint, and serve chilled.

MARROW (SQUASH) RAITA

(Lauki Raita)

Serves 6
Preparation time   15 minutes plus chilling time
Cooking time   10 minutes

This low-calorie side dish is easy to digest and pleases the palate. It tastes better when served chilled, and it's suitable for taking out on picnics. Use a long, green Indian marrow (squash) for this dish.

Imperial (Metric)	American
½ lb (225g) marrow	1 cup squash
Water as necessary	Water as necessary
1 pint (600ml) natural yogurt	2½ cups plain yogurt
Pinch of asafoetida powder (optional)	Dash of asafoetida powder (optional)
Sea salt to taste	Sea salt to taste
½ teaspoon mustard powder	½ teaspoon mustard powder
1 tablespoon green coriander, finely chopped	1 tablespoon cilantro (coriander), finely chopped
½ teaspoon red chilli powder	½ teaspoon red chili powder
1 teaspoon white cumin seeds, roasted and ground	1 teaspoon white cumin seeds, roasted and ground

1

Wash, peel, and grate the marrow (squash) then boil in water to cover until tender. Squeeze out the squash, and set aside.

2

Beat the yogurt and asafoetida until smooth. Add the marrow (squash) together with salt, mustard, and green coriander; blend thoroughly.

3

Garnish with the red chilli and cumin powders, and refrigerate.

4

Serve when needed, straight from the refrigerator.

PUMPKIN RAITA

(Kaddu Raita)

Serves 4	
Preparation time 20 minutes plus chilling time	
Cooking time 10 minutes	

Pumpkin is a very common vegetable in India, and is fairly inexpensive. But the raita made from this common ingredient is deliciously uncommon! Use green baby pumpkin for the best results.

Imperial (Metric)	American
½ lb (225g) green pumpkin	½ pound green pumpkin
Water as needed	Water as needed
½ pint (300ml) natural yogurt	1¼ cups plain yogurt
Sea salt to taste	Sea salt to taste
Pinch of black pepper powder	Dash of black pepper powder
Small pinch of asafoetida powder	Small dash of asafoetida powder
½ teaspoon garam masala	½ teaspoon garam masala
1 tablespoon shredded fresh mint	1 tablespoon shredded fresh mint

1

Wash the pumpkin; remove the outer skin and the stringy substance and seeds from inside. This will reduce the ready weight of the pumpkin to just over ¼ pound (100g). Grate the pumpkin, and then put in water.

2

Carefully wash the grated pumpkin, and then boil until tender. Remove from heat, and let cool, then gently squeeze out the pumpkin and put aside.

3

Beat the yogurt until it assumes a smooth consistency. Stir in the salt, pepper, and asafoetida, and beat again.

4

Add the pumpkin to the yogurt and blend.

5

Garnish with garam masala and shredded mint; chill and serve.

FENUGREEK LEAVES RAITA

(Methi Saag Raita)

Serves 4
Preparation time   20 minutes plus chilling time
Cooking time   10 minutes

Everyone knows that greens are good for you, but if they can be transformed into a tasty dish that adds life to a meal, what more can you ask? This is one such dish — feel free to adapt it to your exact taste.

Imperial (Metric)	American
½ lb (225g) fenugreek leaves	½ pound fenugreek leaves
Water as needed	Water as needed
2 small cartons natural yogurt	2 small cartons plain yogurt
Sea salt to taste	Sea salt to taste
1 tablespoon lemon juice	1 tablespoon lemon juice
Pinch of black pepper powder	Dash of black pepper powder
1 green chilli, chopped	1 green chili, chopped
1 tablespoon green coriander	1 tablespoon green cilantro
1 teaspoon white cumin seeds, roasted and ground	1 teaspoon white cumin seeds, roasted and ground

1

Clean, wash, and wipe the fenugreek; then chop finely. Boil in water until cooked through. Squeeze out the water, and put the fenugreek aside.

2

Whisk the yogurt to a smooth consistency. Stir in the salt, lemon juice, and pepper, and whisk again.

3

Coarsely grind the green chilli and green coriander (cilantro), and add to the yogurt.

4

Add the fenugreek, and blend thoroughly.

5

Garnish with ground cumin, and serve chilled.

SPINACH RAITA

(Paalak Raita)

Serves 6	
Preparation time 20 minutes plus chilling time	
Cooking time 15 minutes	

This is a delicious and cooling side dish that balances a meal if served with other hot dishes. Popeye would be a great fan of this concoction!

Imperial (Metric)	American
1 lb (450g) fresh spinach	1 pound fresh spinach
1 teaspoon ghee	1 teaspoon ghee
1 teaspoon mustard seeds, crushed	1 teaspoon mustard seeds, crushed
1 green chilli, finely chopped	1 green chili, finely chopped
1 pint (600ml) natural yogurt	2½ cups plain yogurt
Sea salt to taste	Sea salt to taste
1 teaspoon red chilli powder	1 teaspoon red chili powder

1

Wash and chop the spinach. Boil in water, drain off, and then grind over the sil-batta.

2

Heat the ghee in a shallow saucepan. Add the mustard seeds and the green chilli, in that order and at an interval of a few seconds. As soon as the mustard starts spitting, add the ground spinach and cook, stirring, about 2 minutes.

3

Meanwhile, beat the yogurt with salt until smooth. Add the spinach mixture, and blend thoroughly.

4

Chilli, serve garnished with the chilli powder.

GREEN CORIANDER RAITA

(Hara Dhaniya Raita)

Serves 6

Preparation time   10 minutes plus chilling time

This concoction is prepared with fresh coriander (cilantro) leaves; unfortunately this aromatic herb is available only in season. Parsley can be substituted as a second best. This preparation will lend colour to your dining table and is sure to whet the appetite.

Imperial (Metric)	American
½ lb (225g) green coriander	½ pound cilantro (coriander)
½ pint (300ml) natural yogurt	1¼ cups plain yogurt
Sea salt to taste	Sea salt to taste
Small pinch of asafoetida powder	Small dash of asafoetida powder
½ teaspoon freshly ground black pepper	½ teaspoon freshly ground black pepper
½ teaspoon garam masala	½ teaspoon garam masala
½ teaspoon red chilli powder	½ teaspoon red chili powder

1

Wash the coriander (cilantro). Discard the stems, and pick just the leaves, chop up and set aside.

2

Beat the yogurt with salt to a smooth consistency. Add asafoetida and pepper, and beat again.

3

Add the coriander (cilantro) to the yogurt, and blend thoroughly.

4

Make a tasteful design on the top of the raita with garam masala and the chilli powder.

5

Refrigerate. Serve straight from refrigerator.

FRESH MINT RAITA

(Podeena Raita)

Serves 4

Preparation time 15 minutes plus chilling time

This raita soothes the eye and pleases the palate. Serve as a side dish with a main meal. The quantity of yogurt and the chilli can be adjusted to taste.

Imperial (Metric)	American
4 oz (100g) fresh mint (leaves)	4 ounces fresh mint (leaves)
1 green chilli	1 green chili
2 small cartons natural yogurt	2 small cartons plain yogurt
1 oz (25g) desiccated coconut	⅓ cup dried coconut
Sea salt to taste	Sea salt to taste
½ teaspoon cumin seeds, roasted and ground	½ teaspoon cumin seeds, roasted and ground
1 teaspoon mustard seeds, coarsely ground	1 teaspoon mustard seeds, coarsely ground

1

Wash and dry the mint and the chilli; then shred finely.

2

Whisk the yogurt to a smooth consistency; add the coconut and salt, and whisk a little more.

3

Add the mint and the chilli, reserving a few shreds of each for later use, to the yogurt mixture and blend thoroughly. Stir in the ground cumin.

4

Garnish with ground mustard and the mint-chilli shreds (saved from earlier on); chill and serve.

CUCUMBER RAITA

(Kakdi Raita)

Serves   6

Preparation time   20 minutes plus chilling time

For the best taste use the Indian variety of baby cucumbers (kheera or kakdi); the commonly available variety will also do. Although considered a delicacy in the West, cucumbers are cheap in India and are readily available during the summer months. Serve chilled with a snack or a full meal.

Imperial (Metric)	American
1 green cucumber (6 oz (175g) ready weight)	1 green cucumber (6 ounces ready weight)
½ pint (300ml) natural yogurt	1¼ cups plain yogurt
Sea salt to taste	Sea salt to taste
Small pinch of asafoetida powder	Small dash of asafoetida powder
1 tablespoon green coriander	1 tablespoon cilantro
1 fresh, green chilli	1 fresh, green chili
½ teaspoon mustard seeds, ground	½ teaspoon mustard seeds, ground
1 teaspoon while cumin seeds, roasted and ground	1 teaspoon while cumin seeds, roasted and ground

1

Wash and dry the cucumber; then chop finely (after scraping or peeling off the outer skin).

2

Whisk the yogurt to a smooth consistency; add the salt and asafoetida, and whisk again.

3

Grind the coriander (cilantro) and green chilli over a sil-batta; stir into the whisked yogurt.

4

Add the cucumber to the yogurt, and blend well.

5

Garnish tastefully with the mustard and cumin powders, chill, and serve.

CARROT RAITA

(Gaajar Raita)

Serves 4

Preparation time 15 minutes plus soaking and chilling time

This concoction gives you an exotic taste from local produce! When ready this raita will be crunchy and will add "muscle" to your meal.

Imperial (Metric)	American
4 medium carrots	4 medium carrots
Water as necessary	Water as necessary
¼ pint (150ml) natural yogurt	⅔ cup plain yogurt
Sea salt to taste	Sea salt to taste
½ teaspoon black pepper powder	½ teaspoon black pepper powder
½ teaspoon lemon juice	½ teaspoon lemon juice
½ teaspoon cumin powder	½ teaspoon cumin powder
1 tablespoon fresh mint, chopped	1 tablespoon fresh mint, chopped

1

Wash and dry the carrots; then grate finely, and soak in warm water 15 to 20 minutes.

2

Meanwhile, whisk the yogurt with salt, pepper, and lemon juice until it attains a smooth consistency.

3

Squeeze out the carrot, and add to the yogurt. Stir in the cumin powder, and blend thoroughly.

4

Garnish with chopped mint, and serve chilled.

BANANA RAITA

(Kela Raita)

Serves 4

Preparation time 10 minutes plus chilling time

This dish is an interesting cross between a traditional raita and a dessert, but it's usually served with the meal. Feel free to adjust the quantities of sugar and chilli to your taste.

Imperial (Metric)	American
2 ripe bananas	2 ripe bananas
½ pint (300ml) natural yogurt	1¼ cups plain yogurt
1 teaspoon raw cane sugar	1 teaspoon raw sugar
½ teaspoon lemon juice	½ teaspoon lemon juice
½ teaspoon sea salt, or to taste	½ teaspoon sea salt, or to taste
½ teaspoon white cumin seeds, roasted and coarsely ground	½ teaspoon white cumin seeds, roasted and coarsely ground
½ teaspoon red chilli powder	½ teaspoon red chili powder

1

Peel the bananas, and cut into thin, round slices.

2

Place the yogurt in a bowl; add the sugar, lemon juice, and salt — in that order — and beat to a smooth consistency.

3

Add the banana, and blend thoroughly.

4

Garnish with ground cumin and chilli powder.

5

Chill and serve.

GRAPE AND SATSUMA RAITA

(Angoor aur Santara Raita)

Serves   6

Preparation time   15 minutes plus chilling time

This has been my favourite raita since childhood and I still love it. You will be fascinated with its versatility, too. It can be served as a normal raita or as a dessert. You may substitute other fruits of your choice.

Imperial (Metric)	American
24 ripe (seedless) white grapes	24 ripe (seedless) white grapes
6 tablespoons mandarin satsuma segments	6 tablespoons mandarin satsuma segments
½ pint (300ml) natural yogurt	1¼ cups plain yogurt
Raw cane sugar as needed	Raw sugar as needed
1 teaspoon sea salt	1 teaspoon sea salt
½ teaspoon green cardamom powder	½ teaspoon green cardamom powder
Large pinch of crushed saffron strands	Large dash of crushed saffron strands
1 teaspoon red chilli powder	1 teaspoon red chili powder

1

Wash the grapes, then halve them and remove any seeds. Add the satsuma without too much syrup (if fresh satsuma is used, use about 4 segments per head; peel the fibrous skin and remove the seeds, then use extra sugar to taste).

2

Beat the yogurt with the sugar to a smooth consistency; add the salt and cardamom powder, and beat again.

3

Add the grape-satsuma mixture to the yogurt, and blend thoroughly; stir in the saffron.

4

Garnish with chilli powder and chill; serve when needed.

BATTER-BEAD RAITA

(Boondi Raita)

Serves 6

Preparation time   10 minutes plus soaking and chilling time

This is a truly exotic yogurt-based side dish; it tastes great anywhere. Boondis (little beads or drops made from a gram flour batter) are available in packets from Asian grocery shops; you can make them at home, too. Serve them with meals or take them on picnics. If the raita is too thick, add a little water.

Imperial (Metric)	American
4 oz (100g) boondi	1 cup boondi
½ pint (300ml) natural yogurt	1¼ cups plain yogurt
Pinch of asafoetida powder	Dash of asafoetida powder
Pinch of ground black pepper	Dash of ground black pepper
Sea salt to taste	Sea salt to taste
½ teaspoon garam masala	½ teaspoon garam masala
½ teaspoon cayenne	½ teaspoon cayenne
1 tablespoon green coriander, shredded	1 tablespoon cilantro (coriander), shredded

1

Soak the boondi in lukewarm water about 15 minutes; then gently squeeze the water out.

2

Meanwhile, whisk the yogurt and asafoetida together. Add the salt, black pepper, and garam masala, and whisk again.

3

Add the boondi to the yogurt, and blend thoroughly.

4

Garnish the raita, according to your taste, with cayenne and coriander; refrigerate.

5

Serve when needed, straight from the refrigerator.

FRITTER RAITA

(Phulori Raita)

Serves 6

Preparation time 20 minutes plus soaking and chilling time

Cooking time 15 minutes

This dish belongs to the family of yogurt-based chaat delicacies. It serves faithfully as a classy side dish in any feast; it can also be eaten on its own. You may substitute a daal powder of your liking for gram flour.

Imperial (Metric)	*American*
4 oz (100g) gram flour (besan)	1 cup gram flour (besan)
Water as necessary	Water as necessary
Sea salt as needed	Sea salt as needed
Ghee for deep frying	Ghee for deep frying
1 pint (600ml) natural yogurt	2½ cups plain yogurt
1 fresh, green chilli, chopped	1 fresh, green chili, chopped
1 teaspoon white cumin seeds, roasted and ground	1 teaspoon white cumin seeds, roasted and ground
½ teaspoon red chilli powder	½ teaspoon red chili powder

1

Place the gram flour in a bowl, and make a medium batter using as much water as is needed. Add a large pinch of salt, and whisk well.

2

Heat ghee in a kadhai, or deep frying pan, to smoking point. Using a spoon, carefully drop 1 teaspoon of batter into the kadhai, then another and another; make 6 or 8 drops at a time. These drops will swell up into amorphous shapes. Turn them over with a stirrer until they are golden all over. Then remove and place on paper towels. These are called "phuloris"; use up all the batter making them. When phuloris are made, soak in water 10 to 15 minutes.

3

Whisk the yogurt, with salt to taste to a smooth consistency. Add the green chilli, and whisk again.

4

Squeeze out the water from the phuloris, and add them to the yogurt. Blend well, taking care not to break the phuloris. Sprinkle with the ground cumin, and garnish with the chilli powder; then refrigerate.

5

Serve straight from the refrigerator when needed.

LOTUS PUFFS RAITA

(Makhaana Raita)

Serves 4
Preparation time 10 minutes plus chilling time
Cooking time 5 minutes

If you are looking for an exotic antidote for the chilli hotness in your meal, this dish is it. And it is easy to digest as well.

Imperial (Metric)	American
2 oz (50g) makhaanas (lotus puffs), crushed	2 ounces makhaanas (lotus puffs), crushed
1 teaspoon ghee	1 teaspoon ghee
Sea salt to taste	Sea salt to taste
½ pint (300ml) natural yogurt	1¼ cups plain yogurt
Pinch of cayenne	Dash of cayenne
2 teaspoons white cumin seeds, roasted and coarsely ground	2 teaspoons white cumin seeds, roasted and coarsely ground

1

Clean and polish the makhaanas before crushing them. Then sauté them in ghee with a pinch of salt.

2

In a deep bowl, beat the yogurt to a smooth consistency; add more salt to taste, and cayenne, and whisk briskly.

3

Stir the makhaanas into the yogurt, and allow to blend.

4

Garnish with ground cumin, and serve chilled.

CASHEW-SULTANA (RAISIN) RAITA

(Kaaju-Kishmish Raita)

Serves 4

Preparation time 15 minutes plus soaking and chilling time

Here is a novelty for even those of you who are no strangers to the raita dish. Delight and surprise your family and friends with this offering. The dish offers wide scope for experimentation. Make a raita dish, for instance, with walnuts, peanuts, or whatever else takes your fancy!

Imperial (Metric)	American
4 oz (100g) plain cashew nuts	⅔ cup plain cashew nuts
1 tablespoon sultanas	1 tablespoon golden raisins
2 small cartons natural yogurt	2 small cartons plain yogurt
1 teaspoon raw cane sugar	1 teaspoon raw sugar
Sea salt to taste	Sea salt to taste
½ teaspoon cumin powder	½ teaspoon cumin powder
1 teaspoon red chilli powder	1 teaspoon red chili powder

1

Clean and dry the cashews, then chop up; similarly, chop the sultanas (raisins) in half. Soak in cold water about 30 minutes.

2

Beat the yogurt to a smooth consistency; stir in the sugar, salt, and cumin powder, and beat again.

3

Add the cashews and sultanas (raisins) to the yogurt, and blend thoroughly.

4

Garnish with the chilli powder, and refrigerate about 30 minutes.

5

Serve when needed, straight from the refrigerator.

PISTACHIO-ALMOND RAITA

(Pishta-Baadaam Raita)

Serves 4

Preparation time 15 minutes plus soaking and chilling time

This is a variation on the general theme of a raita dish made from dried fruits and nuts. There is scope for experimentation. Serve as a side dish with a main meal.

Imperial (Metric)	American
2 tablespoons mixture of sliced pistachios and flaked almonds	2 tablespoons mixture of flaked pistachios and slivered almonds
1½ tablespoons sultanas	2 tablespoons golden raisins
½ pint (300ml) natural yogurt	1¼ cups plain yogurt
Sea salt to taste	Sea salt to taste
Pinch of green cardamom powder	Dash of green cardamom powder
½ teaspoon raw cane sugar	½ teaspoon raw sugar
1 teaspoon white cumin seeds, roasted and ground	1 teaspoon white cumin seeds, roasted and ground
1 tablespoon green coriander, shredded	1 tablespoon cilantro, shredded

1

Soak the nuts and sultanas (raisins) in warm water about 30 minutes.

2

Whisk the yogurt and salt to a smooth consistency. Add the cardamom powder and sugar, and whisk again.

3

Drain off the water from the soaking ingredients, and add them to the yogurt mixture.

4

Garnish with ground cumin and green coriander (cilantro); chill and serve.

Chapter 5

Kachumbers and Salads
(Kachumber aur Salaad)

An Indian meal looks wanting without a plate or bowl of kachumber or salad in sight, irrespective of the climate. The colourful *mélange* of raw, crisp, and cool vegetables and fruits lend character to your dining table. A kachumber or salad (but not both) is normally served as a side dish with a main meal, but for vegetarians on a diet of raw foods these dishes can be served as the main course.

Kachumbers and salads are somewhat similar in that they can both be made from standard or seasonal vegetables and fruits. Kachumbers are made quickly, often by chopping or grating the main ingredient and serving it after the addition of seasoning or lemon juice. The salads take longer to prepare and are usually a combination of a number of ingredients moistened with oil, vinegar, or a creamy sauce (e.g. mayonnaise, French dressing, plain cream, yogurt, or coconut milk) before being seasoned and served on a bed of lettuce.

The annals of Indian cuisine dictate that the dishes in this section should be aspics, which are simple to make and which add colour and taste to a meal. They should be fresh, cool, and crunchy even after the dressing, if any, has been added — so do not be too generous with the dressing, and add it at the very last moment. Wash and soak the greens, herbs, and vegetables in ice cold water for about 15 minutes (this will remove all the sand and grit and will keep the ingredients crisp), then rinse and dry them by shaking and patting with a paper towel or spinning in a salad spinner. To improve the taste of the dishes and render them more satisfying, it is important to chill the ingredients for 30 minutes or more until you are ready to serve.

Although these dishes can be made with one ingredient, like lettuce or cabbage, it will add to the flavour and texture if several greens are used together. Some imagination is called for when selecting and combining the main ingredients. Garnishing is important too, especially if it enhances the looks and taste of the dishes. You may do this simply by sprinkling a little chopped herbs (green coriander [cilantro], mint leaves, or parsley) on the finished preparations, or you can use slices of onion, cucumber, tomato, or green chilli. You might also go in for some fancy garnishing like cheese or carrot balls, capsicum rings, roses made of red radish, or white radish curls.

In the north of India, people make these dishes with raw vegetables and seasoning. In the south the plentiful growth of coconuts ensures its generous use in all their dishes, including kachumbers and salads. The east coast of India boasts of scalding the main ingredients in oil when making their salads; in the western part of India, ingredients are minced or grated and spiced. In central India, they pick the best and most popular items from the whole country to make their own cosmopolitan cuisine!

These dishes are very versatile and lend themselves to variety and experimentation. They can be made according to your wishes and tastes, and with the ingredients of your choice. Serve them to balance a meal, i.e. hot or sweet kachumbers and salads with mild and bland meals and others as an antidote to the accompanying hot dishes of the meal. I hope that my selection of recipes in this section of the book represents variety and that it meets with your approval.

CABBAGE-CUCUMBER KACHUMBER

(Bundgobhi-Kheera Kachumber)

Serves 4
Preparation time   15 minutes plus chilling time

A rather crisp preparation that adds muscle and character to a meal. It should go down well at parties, with snacks, and with other savouries.

Imperial (Metric)	American
4 oz (100g) grated cabbage	1 cup grated cabbage
4 oz (100g) grated cucumber	1 cup grated cucumber
1-inch (2½cm) piece of fresh ginger	1-inch piece of fresh ginger
2 small, green chillies	2 small, green chilies
½ teaspoon mustard seeds, crushed	½ teaspoon mustard seeds, crushed
Sea salt to taste	Sea salt to taste
½ teaspoon red chilli powder	½ teaspoon red chili powder
4 tablespoons lemon juice	⅓ cup lemon juice

1
Place the cabbage and cucumber on a serving dish.

2
Scrape the outer skin off the ginger and then grate it; chop the green chillies also.

3
Sprinkle with the mustard seeds and salt and mix thoroughly; then arrange the mixture on a plate. Add the chilli powder and the lemon juice.

4
Chill, and serve.

RADISH AND CARROT KACHUMBER

(Mooli-Gaajar Kachumber)

Serves 4

Preparation time   15 minutes plus chilling time

Radishes and carrots are a popular side dish with Indian meals. They are inexpensive even by Indian standards, but most delightful concoctions can be made from them. I hope you will love this preparation.

Imperial (Metric)	American
4 medium carrots	4 medium carrots
1 medium, white radish	1 medium, white radish
1 firm, red tomato	1 firm, red tomato
1 green chilli	1 green chili
Pinch of carom seeds	Dash of carom seeds
Sea salt to taste	Sea salt to taste
½ teaspoon red chilli powder	½ teaspoon red chili powder
2 tablespoons chopped green coriander	2 tablespoons chopped cilantro
4 tablespoons lemon juice	(coriander)
	⅓ cup lemon juice

1
Scrape the outer skin off carrots and radish, then grate finely.

2
Finely chop the tomato and the green chilli, then place all the grated and chopped ingredients in a serving bowl.

3
Stir in the carom seeds and the salt together with the chilli powder.

4
Garnish with the coriander (cilantro), and pour the lemon juice over the preparation.

5
Serve chilled.

WATER CHESTNUT KACHUMBER

(Singhara Kachumber)

Serves 4

Preparation time 15 minutes plus chilling time

This is very much a seasonal kachumber, even in India; much depends on when and where the water chestnuts are available. For variety, or as alternatives, you may use boiled potatoes, satsumas, and cucumber. An attractive side dish no matter what's used!

Imperial (Metric)	American
8 peeled water chestnuts	8 peeled water chestnuts
1 medium beetroot	1 medium beet
2 carrots	2 carrots
4 florets cauliflower	4 florets cauliflower
4 tablespoons shredded cabbage	5 tablespoons shredded cabbage
4 red radishes	4 red radishes
Sea salt to taste	Sea salt to taste
1 teaspoon red chilli powder	1 teaspoon red chili powder
1 fresh, juicy lemon	1 fresh, juicy lemon

1

Finely grate the water chestnuts, beetroot (beet), carrots, and cauliflower; place in a serving bowl.

2

Add the cabbage and blend in. Then slice the radish and place decoratively over the preparation.

3

Sprinkle on the salt and chilli powder, and squeeze the lemon all over the kachumber.

4

Serve chilled.

CHEESE AND CAPSICUM KACHUMBER

(Paneer aur Shimla Mirch Kachumber)

Serves 4

Preparation time 15 minutes plus chilling time

The twain of East and West meet in this preparation — in taste as well as looks! Do experiment with alternatives if you feel adventurous enough.

Imperial (Metric)	American
4 tablespoons grated cheese	⅓ cup grated cheese
2 medium capsicums (green peppers)	2 medium capsicums (green peppers)
1 firm, red tomato	1 firm, red tomato
1 green chilli	1 green chili
Small pinch of asafoetida powder	Small dash of asafoetida powder
Pinch of mustard powder	Dash of mustard powder
Sea salt to taste	Sea salt to taste
Large pinch of ground black pepper	Large dash of ground black pepper
2 tablespoons lemon juice	2 tablespoons lemon juice
1 tablespoon chopped green coriander	1 tablespoon chopped cilantro (coriander)

1

Place the cheese in a serving bowl.

2

Wash and wipe the capsicums, tomato, and green chilli, and thinly slice lengthwise. Add to the bowl.

3

Sprinkle on the asafoetida and mustard powders, and then salt and black pepper, and blend the mixture carefully.

4

Pour the lemon juice over the preparation, and garnish with coriander (cilantro).

5

Chill and serve.

ONION AND BEET KACHUMBER

(Pyaaz aur Chukander Kachumber)

Serves	4
Preparation time	10 minutes plus chilling time

This preparation has an exotic taste. Feel free to use spring onions (scallions) instead of ordinary onions, and add green chillies to make it hotter. Serve as a side dish.

Imperial (Metric)	American
1 medium onion	1 medium onion
1 medium beetroot	1 medium beet
Sea salt to taste	Sea salt to taste
½ teaspoon ground black pepper	½ teaspoon ground black pepper
2 tablespoons lemon juice	2 tablespoons lemon juice
1 tablespoon chopped green coriander	1 tablespoon chopped cilantro

1

Clean and wash the onion and beetroot (beet); remove their outer skins and grate finely.

2

Place the grated ingredients on a serving dish; sprinkle the salt and pepper over them and sprinkle over the lemon juice.

3

Garnish with the green coriander (cilantro); chill and serve.

GUAVA AND CUCUMBER KACHUMBER

(Amrood aur Kheera Kachumber)

Serves 4

Preparation time   15 minutes plus chilling time

An exotic kachumber *par excellence*! Although it is supposed to be served with a meal, children and occasionally adults have been known to eat it on its own.

Imperial (Metric)	American
4 small, sweet guavas	4 small, sweet guavas
4 oz (100g) cucumber	1 cup cucumber
1 ripe banana	1 ripe banana
Small pinch of asafoetida powder	Small dash of asafoetida powder
Sea salt to taste	Sea salt to taste
1 teaspoon crushed red chillies	1 teaspoon crushed red chilies
2 tablespoons chopped green coriander	2 tablespoons chopped cilantro
4 tablespoons lemon juice	⅓ cup lemon juice

1

Wash and dry the guavas and cucumber; then chop up. Peel the banana, and chop it up, too.

2

Place the chopped ingredients on a serving dish; add asafoetida, salt, and the red chillies.

3

Sprinkle the coriander (cilantro) over the preparation, and then the lemon juice.

4

Chill, and serve.

CAULIFLOWER-SATSUMA KACHUMBER

(Gobhi-Santara Kachumber)

Serves 4
Preparation time   15 minutes plus chilling time

This kachumber can be a real tongue-teaser! Adjust the quantities to suit your palate; even try alternative ingredients. It is usually served with a meal.

Imperial (Metric)	American
4 oz (100g) cauliflower florets	¾ cup cauliflower florets
1 good-sized juicy satsuma	1 good-sized juicy satsuma
1 firm, red tomato	1 firm, red tomato
Sea salt to taste	Sea salt to taste
1 teaspoon red chilli powder	1 teaspoon red chili powder
2 tablespoons shredded white cabbage	2 tablespoons shredded white cabbage
4 tablespoons lemon juice	⅓ cup lemon juice

1

Wash and dry the cauliflower; then grate it. Peel and clean the satsuma segments; remove the skin and seeds, and chop them. Chop tomato also.

2

Place the grated and chopped ingredients on a serving dish; sprinkle with the sea salt and chilli powder.

3

Top the preparation with the shredded cabbage, and sprinkle on the lemon juice.

4

Serve chilled.

CAPSICUM AND RADISH KACHUMBER

(Shimla Mirch aur Mooli Kachumber)

Serves 6

Preparation time 15 minutes plus chilling time

This preparation should be fresh and crunchy when served. Serve chilled as a side dish with a main meal; it can also be served with selected snacks.

Imperial (Metric)	American
4 oz (100g) white radishes	¼ pound white radishes
3 capsicums (green peppers)	3 capsicums (green peppers)
2 green chillies (optional)	2 green chilies (optional)
Sea salt and black pepper powder to taste	Sea salt and black pepper powder to taste
3 small red radishes	3 small red radishes
2 tablespoons lemon juice	2 tablespoons lemon juice
1 tablespoon shredded green mint	1 tablespoon shredded green mint

1

Wash, and dry the radishes and capsicums. Cut the radishes into thin round slices; similarly, cut the capsicums into thin rings. Chop the chillies too, if used.

2

Arrange these on a serving dish, and sprinkle with the salt and black pepper.

3

Slice the red radishes and place them strategically on the serving dish so that their red colour shows through.

4

Sprinkle the lemon juice over the dish, and garnish with the mint.

5

Chill, and serve when required.

ONION-TOMATO KACHUMBER

(Pyaaz-Mamaatar Kachumber)

Serves 6

Preparation time 15 minutes plus chilling time

Use spring onions (scallions) for this dish for best results; ordinary onions can be used also. Make it fresh, and give it a quick chill; do not keep it for too long.

Imperial (Metric)	American
6 spring onions	6 scallions
3 firm, red tomatoes	3 firm, red tomatoes
1 green chilli	1 green chili
1 tablespoon lemon juice	1 tablespoon lemon juice
Sea salt to taste	Sea salt to taste
Pinch of red chilli powder	Dash of red chili powder
2 tablespoons chopped green coriander	2 tablespoons chopped cilantro

1

Wash and dry the onions, tomatoes, and the chilli; then chop finely.

2

Place the chopped ingredients in a serving bowl; add the lemon juice and salt, and blend well.

3

Top with the chilli powder and coriander (cilantro).

4

Serve with or without chilling.

GINGER-CHILLI KACHUMBER

(Adrak-Mirch Kachumber)

Serves 6
Preparation time   10 minutes plus chilling time

This is the easiest of kachumbers to make, but it is meant only for the chilli lovers! Not recommended for children and those with a delicate tongue.

Imperial (Metric)	American
4 green chillies	4 green chilies
3 oz (75g) fresh ginger	3 ounces fresh ginger
2 tablespoons lemon juice	2 tablespoons lemon juice
Sea salt to taste	Sea salt to taste
½ teaspoon freshly ground black pepper	½ teaspoon freshly milled black pepper

1

Wash and dry the chillies; then chop finely. Similarly, wash and dry the ginger; scrape its outer skin, and cut into very fine slices.

2

Place the chillies and ginger in a serving bowl; add the lemon juice, and stir well.

3

Sprinkle the salt and pepper over the mixture, and blend thoroughly.

4

Chill, and serve as a side dish with a meal.

MARROW (SQUASH) SALAD

(Lauki Salaad)

Serves 4

Preparation time 20 minutes plus chilling time

Use a long Indian marrow (squash) for this preparation. A lightweight concoction which will titillate your taste buds no end! Usually served as a side dish with a main meal.

Imperial (Metric)	American
½ lb (225g) baby marrow	1 cup baby squash
4 mushrooms	4 mushrooms
4 oz (100g) white radish	¼ pound white radish
1 tablespoon olive oil	1 tablespoon olive oil
4 tablespoons lemon juice	⅓ cup lemon juice
2 cloves garlic, crushed	2 cloves garlic, crushed
Sea salt to taste	Sea salt to taste
½ teaspoon cayenne	½ teaspoon cayenne
½ teaspoon garam masala	½ teaspoon garam masala
8 crisp lettuce leaves	8 crisp lettuce leaves
1 red and firm tomato, sliced	1 red and firm tomato, sliced
1 medium green pepper, cut into rings	1 medium green pepper, cut into rings

1

Peel the marrow (squash), and shred it into strips, discarding the core.

2

Wash and dry the mushrooms and radish; slice finely.

3

Make a mixture of olive oil, lemon juice, and garlic; add to marrow (squash), mushrooms, and radish. Sprinkle on the salt, cayenne, and garam masala and mix thoroughly.

4

Combine this spiced mixture with the lettuce, tomato, and green pepper, and chill in a refrigerator about 1 hour.

5

Make a bed of lettuce in a large serving bowl or dish, and place the spiced vegetable mixture on it. Garnish with slices of tomato and green pepper and serve.

PEAR SALAD

(Naashpaati Salaad)

Serves 4

Preparation time 15 minutes plus soaking and chilling time

This exotic concoction will be a sure hit with children; serve as a side dish with a main meal. Goes down well with bland meals.

Imperial (Metric)	American
8 lettuce leaves	8 lettuce leaves
4 medium pears	4 medium pears
4 cauliflower florets	4 cauliflower florets
4 mushrooms	4 mushrooms
4 oz (100g) fresh cream cheese	½ cup fresh cream cheese
1 beetroot	1 beet
1 medium onion	1 medium onion
Thick orange juice to coat	Thick orange juice to coat
2 tablespoons French dressing	2 tablespoons French dressing
Sea salt to taste	Sea salt to taste
½ teaspoon each of cayenne and garam masala	½ teaspoon each of cayenne and garam masala

1

Soak the lettuce in ice-cold water 15 to 20 minutes to remove the grit and dirt; then drain off the water, pat the lettuce dry, and refrigerate.

2

Peel the pears, and halve them; remove the cores.

3

Grate the cauliflower and mushrooms, and add the cheese; also grate the beetroot (beet) and onion. Then refrigerate all of these and the pear at least 30 minutes, or until about to serve.

4

On a large serving dish, spread out the lettuce leaves and neatly arrange the pear halves over them, but only after brushing with orange juice.

5

Mix together the cauliflower, mushrooms, cheese and French Dressing. Sprinkle the preparation with the salt, cayenne, and garam masala. Garnish with the grated beetroot (beet) and onion, and serve as needed.

CHEESE AND ONION SALAD

(Paneer aur Pyaaz Salaad)

Serves 4

Preparation time 20 minutes plus soaking and chilling time

A distinctive salad that combines taste with looks; it also lends itself to experimentation with alternatives. It should prove a popular side dish with friends and relatives.

Imperial (Metric)	American
8 crisp lettuce leaves	8 crisp lettuce leaves
½ lb (225g) fresh cream cheese	1 cup fresh cream cheese
1 large onion	1 large onion
2 sticks celery	2 stalks celery
1 green chilli	1 green chili
1 medium tomato	1 medium tomato
4 red radishes	4 red radishes
4 tablespoons salad cream or mayonnaise	⅓ cup mayonnaise
Sea salt to taste	Sea salt to taste
1 teaspoon mustard seeds, crushed	1 teaspoon mustard seeds, crushed

1

Soak the lettuce in ice-cold water about 15 minutes; then take out from water, and refrigerate in a plastic bag.

2

Chop the cheese, onion, and celery; similarly, chop the green chilli, cut the tomato into wedges, and slice the radishes. Then place the cheese and all the vegetables in the refrigerator for at least 30 minutes. Take them out when you are ready to serve.

3

Line a large, glass serving bowl with the lettuce. Dress the cheese, onion, and celery with salad cream (or mayonnaise), and place over the lettuce; then sprinkle on the green chilli, salt, and mustard.

4

Garnish with tomato and radish, and serve as needed.

CABBAGE SALAD

(Bundgobhi Salaad)

Serves 4

Preparation time 20 minutes plus soaking and chilling time

This salad should be crunchy and tasty when served; it is bound to enhance the general tone of any meal! Do try it with your own alternative ingredients, if you wish, and delight your friends with your prowess.

Imperial (Metric)	American
8 crisp lettuce leaves	8 crisp lettuce leaves
4 oz (100g) white cabbage	¼ pound white cabbage
1 large green pepper	1 large green pepper
1 stick celery	1 stalk celery
1 onion	1 onion
4 canned pineapple rings	4 canned pineapple rings
2 tablespoons chopped green coriander	2 tablespoons chopped cilantro
Pinch of asafoetida powder	(coriander)
1 tablespoon olive oil	Dash of asafoetida powder
1 teaspoon mustard seeds, crushed	1 tablespoon olive oil
4 tablespoons sour cream	1 teaspoon mustard seeds, crushed
Sea salt to taste	⅓ cup sour cream
1 teaspoon cumin powder	Sea salt to taste
	1 teaspoon cumin powder

1

Soak the lettuce, cabbage, green pepper, and celery in ice-cold water about 30 minutes; then drain off the water and pat dry with a paper towel.

2

Finely grate the cabbage, green pepper, celery, and onion, chop up the pineapple rings. Then refrigerate these, together with the lettuce and coriander, at least 30 minutes, or until ready to serve. Make a bed of lettuce on a large serving dish.

3

Mix the cabbage, green pepper, celery, onion, and pineapple with asafoetida and olive oil. Place the mixture over the lettuce, and sprinkle the crushed mustard over the preparation.

4

Dress the mixture with sour cream, and add salt and cumin powder. Serve when needed, topped with green coriander (cilantro).

THREE C's SALAD

(Sabzi Salaad)

Serves 6

Preparation time   20 minutes plus soaking and chilling time

This colourful salad soothes the eye and pleases the palate. Substitute cucumber or cabbage for one of the main ingredients, and you will still have a 3 C's salad! Then you may prepare the vegetables differently — chop or grate them.

Imperial (Metric)	American
12 fresh lettuce leaves	12 fresh lettuce leaves
3 sticks celery	3 stalks celery
3 plump carrots	3 plump carrots
3 small capsicums (green peppers)	3 small capsicums (green peppers)
1 small onion	1 small onion
6 red radishes	6 red radishes
3 fresh but long green chillies	3 fresh but long green chilies
Sea salt to taste	Sea salt to taste
1½ cloves garlic, crushed	1½ cloves garlic, crushed
3 tablespoons cider vinegar	¼ cup cider vinegar
1 teaspoon raw cane sugar	1 teaspoon raw sugar

1

Soak the lettuce in cold water; then drain off the water and refrigerate the leaves until ready to serve.

2

Chop the celery, carrots, and capsicums in such a way that you have long strips of them rather like sticks. Peel and cut the onion into rings, and slice the red radishes. Cut the green chillies into sticklike strips, too. Then refrigerate them all at least 30 minutes, or until about to be served.

3

Place 2 lettuce leaves on each serving dish (have 6 ready); then arrange the celery, carrots, and capsicum (green pepper) on them, and position the green chilli strips strategically on each plate. Sprinkle the salt over the preparation.

4

Make a liquid mixture from the garlic, vinegar and sugar, and sprinkle it over each serving. Garnish the salad plates with onion rings and radish slices, adding more salt as needed, and serve when needed.

FRESH FRUIT SALAD

(Taaze Phalon ka Salaad)

Serves 4

Preparation time 15 minutes plus soaking and chilling time

This is a delicious salad; it goes well as a side dish with a bland meal like boiled rice and plain daal. It clearly offers a choice of different and/or seasonal fruits.

Imperial (Metric)	American
8 crisp lettuce leaves	8 crisp lettuce leaves
4 peaches	4 peaches
1 ripe banana	1 ripe banana
20 seedless grapes	20 seedless grapes
4 tablespoons diced pineapple flesh	4 tablespoons diced pineapple flesh
2 tablespoons chopped green coriander	2 tablespoons chopped cilantro
4 tablespoons single cream, to dress	⅓ cup light cream, to dress
Sea salt to taste	Sea salt to taste
½ teaspoon each of black pepper and red chilli powders	½ teaspoon each of black pepper and red chili powders
1 tablespoon fresh lemon juice	1 tablespoon fresh lemon juice

1

Soak the lettuce in cold water about 15 minutes. Then shake and pat dry with a paper towel; put in a plastic bag, and refrigerate at least 30 minutes.

2

Clean the peaches, and dice their flesh, discarding the stones. Peel the banana and chop it up; halve the grapes. Then refrigerate the fruit, including pineapple, 30 minutes (with lettuce), together with the green coriander.

3

Arrange 2 lettuce leaves on each of four serving dishes, and neatly position the prepared fruit on them

4

Dress with cream, and sprinkle the seasoning on each serving.

5

Serve when needed, sprinkling with lemon juice and topping with coriander (cilantro).

POTATO AND RADISH SALAD

(Aalu aur Mooli Salaad)

Serves 6

Preparation time   15 minutes plus soaking and chilling time

This preparation should please everyone because it offers scope for alternatives; instead of potato, you may use satsuma. Serve in the company of pickles with a main meal or with a snack. Vinegar could be replaced with sour cream or lemon juice.

Imperial (Metric)	American
12 lettuce leaves	12 lettuce leaves
6 medium potatoes, boiled	6 medium potatoes, boiled
½ lb (225g) white radish	½ pound white radish
6 cauliflower florets	6 cauliflower florets
2 small green chillies	2 small green chilies
3 medium carrots	3 medium carrots
2 tablespoons chopped, green coriander (or parsley)	2 tablespoons chopped cilantro (or parsley)
Pinch of asafoetida powder	Dash of asafoetida powder
Sea salt to taste	Sea salt to taste
1½ teaspoons cumin powder	1½ teaspoons cumin powder
2 tablespoons cider vinegar	3 tablespoons cider vinegar
1 teaspoon raw cane sugar (optional)	1 teaspoon raw sugar (optional)

1
Soak the lettuce in cold water about 15 minutes; then dry and put in a plastic bag.

2
Dice the potato, radish, cauliflower, green chilli, and carrots. Then place all these ingredients, together with the lettuce and coriander, in the refrigerator at least 30 minutes, or until ready to serve.

3
Take out, and place 2 lettuce leaves on each of the 6 serving plates; then neatly arrange the diced vegetables on the lettuce.

4
Add a dash of asafoetida, salt, and cumin powder to each serving.

5
Pour the vinegar over each portion of salad, and add sugar. Serve sprinkled with the coriander (cilantro).

BEETROOT AND CUCUMBER SALAD

(Chukander aur Kheera Salaad)

Serves 6

Preparation time   15 minutes plus soaking and chilling time

This concoction is colourful and palatable. Serve it as a crisp side dish in the company of, or instead of, a raita or chutney.

Imperial (Metric)	American
12 lettuce leaves	12 lettuce leaves
2 medium beetroot	2 medium beets
6 oz (175g) cucumber	1 small cucumber
6 spring onions	6 scallions
3 tablespoons chopped, fresh mint	3 tablespoons chopped, fresh mint
Mayonnaise to dress	Mayonnaise to dress
Sea salt to taste	Sea salt to taste
1 teaspoon garam masala	1 teaspoon garam masala

1

Soak the lettuce in cold water for 15 minutes to remove the grit and dirt; shake, pat dry, and put in a plastic bag.

2

Finely grate the beetroot (beets), cucumber, and spring onions (scallions); and then place them, together with the lettuce and mint, in the refrigerator at least 30 minutes, or until about to serve.

3

Take out from the refrigerator, and place 2 lettuce leaves on each serving dish (prepare 6 of them). Arrange the beetroot (beet), cucumber, and onion on them.

4

Dress with mayonnaise, and sprinkle each serving with the salt and garam masala.

5

Serve when needed, topped with the chopped mint.

ONION AND SATSUMA SALAD

(Pyaaz aur Santara Salaad)

Serves   4

Preparation time   15 minutes plus soaking and chilling time

If a salad looks attractive, and tastes to match, no one can refuse your offer even if they have no room left! Serve chilled and crisp.

Imperial (Metric)	American
8 lettuce leaves	8 lettuce leaves
2 small onions	2 small onions
2 medium carrots	2 medium carrots
4 oz (100g) cucumber	1 small cucumber
4 tablespoons chopped satsuma flesh	⅓ cup chopped satsuma flesh
Whisked single cream to dress	Whisked light cream to dress
Sea salt and pepper to taste	Sea salt and pepper to taste
4 tablespoons shredded cabbage	4 tablespoons shredded cabbage

1

Wash and soak the lettuce in ice-cold water for about 20 minutes; then shake and pat dry, and put in a plastic bag.

2

Grate the onion, carrots, and cucumber; then place them all, together with lettuce leaves and satsuma in the refrigerator for at least 30 minutes, or until ready to serve.

3

Place 2 lettuce leaves on each serving dish. Neatly arrange onion, carrots, cucumber, and satsuma on it.

4

Dress with cream (use sour cream if desired); sprinkle salt and pepper on each serving.

5

Garnish with cabbage and serve when needed.

PIMENTO AND PINEAPPLE SALAD

(Shimla Mirch aur Anannas Salaad)

Serves   6

Preparation time   15 minutes plus soaking and chilling time

Make sure that all ingredients are cleaned, washed, and refrigerated; take them out just before serving. If your greens are fresh and crisp at the time of eating, your preparation will be a success!

Imperial (Metric)	American
2 medium pimentoes	2 medium pimentoes
6 tablespoons chopped pineapple	½ cup chopped pineapple
2 tablespoons grated cheese	3 tablespoons grated cheese
3 firm, red tomatoes	3 firm, red tomatoes
12 lettuce leaves	12 lettuce leaves
2 tablespoons chopped, green coriander	2 tablespoons chopped cilantro
Sea salt to taste	Sea salt to taste
½ teaspoon red chili powder	½ teaspoon red chili powder
2 tablespoons lemon juice (or dressing of your choice)	2 tablespoons lemon juice (or dressing of your choice)
1 teaspoon raw cane sugar	1 teaspoon raw sugar

1
Wash the pimentoes, then chop them and the pineapple. Cut the tomatoes into wedges.

2
Clean, then soak the lettuce in cold water at least 10 minutes to remove all the dirt and grit; then put in a plastic bag.

3
Put all these ingredients, including washed, soaked, and chopped coriander (cilantro), into the refrigerator at least 30 minutes.

4
Just before serving, take out all the ingredients from the refrigerator. Place 2 lettuce leaves on each serving plate, and arrange pimento, pineapple, cheese, and tomato on them. Sprinkle salt and chilli powder over them, and pour lemon juice and sugar on top.

5
Garnish each plate with chopped coriander (cilantro), and serve.

Chapter 6

Pickles
(Achaar)

A pickle with an Indian meal is like make-up on the face of a pretty girl: it makes her even more ravishing, and the pickle makes you even more ravenous! Like not overusing make-up, pickles, in order to have their fullest impact, must be served in small quantities. Pickles prod sluggish appetites and aid digestion; they form an integral part of a meal and are served regularly with snacks. Because of their pungency and contrasting flavours, they liven up any meal and team up felicitously with boiled and plain food. All pickles tend to tickle the palate, enhance the flavour of the meal, and bring colour to your table.

Indians have been making pickles for centuries and are the acknowledged experts in that field. In consequence, Indian pickles are a world in themselves, and a truly bewildering variety of them are made in that country. They are made in many different ways but are basically of two persuasions: sour, and sweet or sweet-and-sour. Pickles can be mild and sweet, sour and tangy, or hot and spicy, depending upon your mood and liking and upon the guests you are serving. Many pickles are instant and can be made very quickly; they should not be kept for more than a few days. Some, prepared and matured over a couple of days or so, last a few weeks. Others, which may take up to two weeks to mature, can easily last two or three months. Finally, there are pickles which take roughly a year to mature and last almost forever; unfortunately these pickles require excruciating care and caution. Given that very few have that much time to spare these days, I have omitted this last category of pickles.

Like chutneys, pickles are made from fruits, vegetables, and dried fruits and nuts. Almost every vegetable and fruit under the sun is pickled one way or another in some part of India. The preserving and pickling agents used in India are salt, oil, lemon juice, vinegar, and spices, or a combination of two or more. They all keep the main fruit or vegetable ingredient from going bad and play their own part in shaping and maintaining the taste, flavour and looks of the pickles. Most of the longer-lasting pickles are made in oil. Although any vegetable oil can be used, the most popular is mustard oil because of the colour and flavour it brings to the pickle. The sweet pickles have sugar or molasses added to them, as prescribed in specific recipes. Most pickles are ready more quickly, last longer, and acquire a fuller taste if exposed to direct sunlight. The longer-lasting pickles require constant and sustained sunshine over a long period. However, for the sun-starved parts of the West, other expedients are recommended — say the warmest place in the house (but then the pickles take longer to mature) — or heating up the liquid pickling agent before use. Many Indian pickles, like wines, mature with time and attain a pinnacle of perfection in flavour and taste.

Certain points should be carefully noted when making pickles. The main vegetable and fruit ingredients should always be fresh, and the dried fruits and nuts should be in prime condition. They should normally be washed and dried before being sliced, shredded, or mashed. Unless it is a boiling pickle, the main ingredient should only be parboiled (and not fully cooked) before being pickled. The basic steps given in the recipes should be followed religiously. When ready, the pickle should be stored in a clean, dry, and sterilized jar, bottle, or crock; the mouth of the container should be covered with a lid or a clean cloth. Whenever possible, pickles should be exposed to direct sunlight, even if they are quick or short life span pickles. Wooden spatulas are ideal for handling all types of pickles while stirring or storing them; otherwise use clean and dry spoons when serving pickles, and be sure to clean them afterwards.

SOUR PICKLES

(Khatte Achaar)

PICKLED CARROTS

(Gaajar ka Achaar)

| Serves | 10 helpings or more |
| Preparation time | 10 minutes |

This is an instant pickle and can be served as soon as it is made. Feel free to put it out in the sun for two or three days, to make it last a little longer. This pickle can also be made with lemon juice or vinegar instead of oil, or with turnips or green chillies instead of carrots.

Imperial (Metric)	American
1 lb (450g) carrots	4 medium carrots
1 teaspoon sea salt (or to taste)	1 teaspoon sea salt (or to taste)
1 teaspoon red chilli powder	1 teaspoon red chili powder
1 tablespoon mustard seeds, crushed	1 tablespoon mustard seeds, crushed
1 tablespoon mango powder (amchoor)	1 tablespoon mango powder (amchoor)
6 tablespoons mustard oil	½ cup mustard oil
Large pinch of asafoetida powder	Large dash of asafoetida powder
1 teaspoon turmeric powder	1 teaspoon turmeric powder

1

Wash the carrots; then slice into thin, long sticks.

2

Add the salt, chilli powder, mustard, and mango powder to the carrots and mix well.

3

Heat the oil in a frying pan, and sauté the asafoetida and turmeric powder over moderate heat about 2 minutes.

4

Pour the oil over the carrots, and blend thoroughly. Serve as needed. Store the leftovers in a clean, lidded jar. Cover the lid after each use, and keep the jar in a warm place.

SAUTÉED CHILLI PICKLE

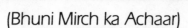

(Bhuni Mirch ka Achaar)

Serves 20 helpings or more
Preparation time 20 minutes
Cooking time 10 minutes

This is a truly instant pickle. Serve it hot or cold soon after it is made. It is made very quickly, too. It is most conveniently made when you are cooking stuffed vegetables; it takes the same stuffing, and the pickle is cooked almost without effort. If you have the spices ready, you may make the pickle whenever you buy green chillies!

Imperial (Metric)	American
½ lb (225g) fresh, green chillies	½ pound fresh, green chilies
A pinch each of nigella and fenugreek seeds	A dash each of nigella and fenugreek seeds
2 teaspoons each of coriander seeds and mango powder	2 teaspoons each of coriander seeds and mango powder
1 teaspoon fennel	1 teaspoon fennel
Large pinch of sea salt (or to taste)	Large dash of sea salt (or to taste)
1 tablespoon mustard oil	1 tablespoon mustard oil

1

Wipe the chillies with a damp cloth. Keeping their stalks, slit them lengthwise (or remove the stalks and discard them), and scoop out the insides.

2

Dry-roast the ingredients, as listed from nigella to sea salt, for 2 to 3 minutes in a frying pan, then grind them. Add the chilli flesh and 2 teaspoons oil, and mix thoroughly.

3

Fill the chillies with this stuffing. Any leftover spice mixture should be spread over the chillies when they are cooking.

4

Heat the remaining oil in a frying pan; position the stuffed chillies in the pan, cover it, and cook over moderate heat 2 to 3 minutes. Then open the lid, turn the chillies over, put the lid back on, and cook for another 2 to 3 minutes.

5

Remove pan from heat, and serve the pickle hot or cold.

PICKLED SATSUMAS

(Santare ka Achaar)

Serves	*40 helpings or more*
Preparation time	*15 minutes*
Cooking time	*20 minutes*

This is another instant pickle made by boiling. It has a typical tangy, exotic taste. You may try making a similar pickle with another juicy citrus fruit. It injects new life into an otherwise dull meal; serve with western meals, too.

Imperial (Metric)	American
12 juicy satsumas	12 juicy satsumas
Pinch of asafoetida powder	Dash of asafoetida powder
1 tablespoon coriander seeds, crushed	1 tablespoon coriander seeds, crushed
4 cloves, crushed	4 cloves, crushed
1 tablespoon garam masala	1 tablespoon garam masala
Sea salt to taste	Sea salt to taste
2 teaspoons red chilli powder	2 teaspoons red chili powder
6 tablespoons lemon juice	½ cup lemon juice

1

Peel satsumas and cut them into four sections, but holding together at the bottom like a flower, and remove the seeds.

2

Place the satsumas in a saucepan. Sprinkle on all the spices and seasoning — from asafoetida to red chilli powder — and put over moderate heat about 10 minutes.

3

Add the lemon juice, together with any additional salt (or black salt, if you wish), and bring the mixture to a slow boil — about 10 minutes.

4

Remove pan from heat, and serve hot or cold. Store in a clean jar or bottle for later use. You may put it out in the sun for a while if you wish.

BABACO PICKLE

(Kamrakh ka Achaar)

Serves	*20 helpings or more*
Preparation time	*15 minutes plus maturing time*

This pickle can also be made with lemon juice instead of oil if you prefer. It's a good side dish to have round to perk up a meal; besides, it is almost instant — ready to serve the day after it is made.

Imperial (Metric)	*American*
8 small babacoes	8 small babacoes
Sea salt to taste	Sea salt to taste
1 teaspoon turmeric powder	1 teaspoon turmeric powder
1 tablespoon mustard seeds	1 tablespoon mustard seeds
1 teaspoon each of white cumin and fenugreek seeds	1 teaspoon each of white cumin and fenugreek seeds
1 tablespoon coriander seeds	1 tablespoon coriander seeds
2 teaspoons cayenne	2 teaspoons cayenne
¼ pint (150ml) mustard oil	⅔ cup mustard oil

1

Wipe the babacoes with a damp cloth; cut them into four slices lengthwise, removing the bitter centre.

2

Take the next seven ingredients, as listed (from salt to cayenne), and grind them together coarsely.

3

Heat the oil, and add to the ground spice mixture to make a paste.

4

Smear the babaco slices with this paste; put them in a jar and out in the sun for a day. This should be ready to serve the next day.

5

Shake the jar before each use, and cover it soon afterwards.

PICKLED RADISH

(Mooli ka Achaar)

Serves	10 helpings or more
Preparation time	15 minutes plus maturing time

Use the long white radish for this pickle — they are now available even in supermarkets! Make large quantities if needed, but do not make more than to last 2 to 3 weeks. Serve as a side dish with a main meal.

Imperial (Metric)	American
1 lb (450g) white radish	1 pound white radish
1 tablespoon sea salt (or to taste)	1 tablespoon sea salt (or to taste)
1 teaspoon turmeric powder	1 teaspoon turmeric powder
2 tablespoons mustard oil	2 tablespoons mustard oil
1 teaspoon garam masala	1 teaspoon garam masala
1 teaspoon each of fenugreek, coriander, and mustard seeds, coarsely ground	1 teaspoon each of fenugreek, coriander, and mustard seeds, coarsely ground
1 teaspoon red chilli powder	1 teaspoon red chili powder
½ pint (300ml) lemon juice	1¼ cups lemon juice

1

Wash and pat the radish dry; scrape its outer skin, and then slice the radish into serving-sized pieces.

2

Add salt and turmeric to the radish, and blend thoroughly. Put the mixture in a suitably sized lidded glass jar.

3

Heat the oil, and sauté the garam masala and other coarsely ground spices 5 minutes over medium heat. Remove from the heat; pour, when a little cool, over the radish, and mix carefully.

4

Sprinkle on the chilli powder, add the lemon juice, cover, and put the jar out in the sun for 2 to 3 days; shake the jar at least once a day.

5

Serve when needed; cover after each use.

CAULIFLOWER PICKLE

(Gobhi ka Achaar)

Serves	*10 helpings*
Preparation time	*15 minutes plus parboiling and maturing time*

You can make this pickle with an alternative vegetable of your liking such as turnip or potato. It can also be made with vinegar or lemon juice instead of oil.

Imperial (Metric)	American
1 lb (450g) cauliflower, ready weight	1 pound cauliflower, ready weight
1 tablespoon sea salt (or to taste)	1 tablespoon sea salt (or to taste)
1 tablespoon each of coriander seeds and fennel	1 tablespoon each of coriander seeds and fennel
1 teaspoon fenugreek seeds	1 teaspoon fenugreek seeds
1 teaspoon turmeric powder	1 teaspoon turmeric powder
2 teaspoons mango powder (amchoor)	2 teaspoons mango powder (amchoor)
¼ pint (150ml) mustard oil	⅔ cup mustard oil

1

Wash and cut the cauliflower into medium-sized pieces. Parboil in water; drain off, sprinkle with 1 teaspoon sea salt, and leave to dry.

2

Dry roast the coriander, fennel, and fenugreek seeds on a griddle, and coarsely grind them; mix with turmeric and mango powders.

3

Place the cauliflower in a glass jar, add the spice mixture and the remaining salt (as desired), and stir thoroughly.

4

Drop in the oil, and shake the jar to blend the ingredients. Cover the jar with a lid or muslin cloth and put it out in the sun (or the warmest place in the house) for 2 to 3 days. Alternatively, heat the oil before use.

5

Shake the jar at least once a day; cover it after each use.

PICKLED GREEN PEAS

(Hari Matar ka Achaar)

Serves	*20 helpings or more*
Preparation time	*20 minutes plus maturing time*

Freshly shelled peas are, of course, ideal for this pickle, but frozen peas will do. Use a vegetable oil of your choice, if mustard oil does not suit you. Anyone can make this pickle, and everyone likes it!

Imperial (Metric)	American
1 lb (450g) shelled peas	2⅔ cups shelled peas
½ pint (300ml) mustard oil	1¼ cups mustard oil
1 teaspoon each of fennel, fenugreek and carom seeds, lightly pounded	1 teaspoon each of fennel, fenugreek and carom seeds, lightly pounded
1 teaspoon each of turmeric and mango powders	1 teaspoon each of turmeric and mango powders
½ teaspoon asafoetida powder	½ teaspoon asafoetida powder
1 tablespoon sea salt (or to taste)	1 tablespoon sea salt (or to taste)
1 tablespoon pounded red chillies	1 tablespoon pounded red chilies

1

Boil enough water to cover the peas. Remove the pan from the heat, and put the peas in. Drain off the water 2 minutes later, and let the peas dry.

2

Heat 2 tablespoons oil in a frying pan, and sauté the pounded and powdered spices for 5 minutes. Remove the frying pan from the heat and let it cool a little.

3

Sprinkle the asafoetida at the base of a clean crock. Drop in the peas first, then the sautéed spices over them.

4

Sprinkle the salt and red chillies over the mixture; pour in the remaining oil, cover the crock with a cloth (or lid), and put it out in the hot sun for 2 to 3 days.

5

Serve as needed, covering the crock after each use.

PICKLED PUMPKIN

(Kaddu ka Achaar)

Serves	*15 helpings or more*
Preparation time	*20 minutes plus maturing time*
Cooking time	*15 minutes*

This is a rather unusual pickle. For best results use green pumpkin rather than the yellow grandfather variety. I am sure this preparation will bring a welcome change in the flavour of your meal. It can be made with lemon juice or vinegar, too.

Imperial (Metric)	*American*
1 lb (450g) green pumpkin	1 pound green pumpkin
1 teaspoon each of white cumin, carom, coriander and fenugreek seeds	1 teaspoon each of white cumin, carom, coriander and fenugreek seeds
¼ teaspoon turmeric powder	¼ teaspoon turmeric powder
2 tablespoons mango powder (amchoor)	2 tablespoons mango powder (amchoor)
8 black peppercorns	8 black peppercorns
1 teaspoon garam masala	1 teaspoon garam masala
Sea salt to taste	Sea salt to taste
2 tablespoons lemon juice	2 tablespoons lemon juice
6 tablespoons mustard oil	½ cup mustard oil

1
Wash and dry the pumpkin. Cut it into thin, long slices, coring the middle. Parboil in water; then drain off the water, and let the pumpkin dry in a cool place.

2
Dry-roast all the ingredients listed, from white cumin to salt, over a griddle for 2 to 3 minutes; grind them together and, using the lemon juice, make a paste.

3
Smear the paste over the pumpkin slices, and put the slices in a clean, dry, and sterilized glass jar with a lid.

4
Heat the oil; then let it cool and pour it over the pumpkin slices. Cover the jar, and place it outside in the sun for 3 to 4 days, taking it indoors during the night. Shake the jar at least once a day.

5
Serve as needed. Cover the lid soon after use, and do not leave the serving spoon or spatula inside the jar.

AUBERGINE (EGGPLANT) PICKLE

(Baigan ka Achaar)

Serves	10 helpings or more
Preparation time	15 minutes plus maturing time
Cooking time	20 minutes

Use thin, long, and seedless black aubergines (eggplants) for this pickle, not the fat, round variety. This pickle is ready relatively quickly, but do not keep it for much longer than a couple of weeks. Do experiment with your own alternatives.

Imperial (Metric)	American
4 medium aubergines	4 medium eggplants
½ teaspoon turmeric powder	½ teaspoon turmeric powder
Sea salt to taste	Sea salt to taste
1 pint (600ml) mustard oil	2½ cups mustard oil
4 cloves garlic, chopped	4 cloves garlic, chopped
1 teaspoon sliced root ginger	1 teaspoon sliced root ginger
1 tablespoon each of mango powder and garam masala	1 tablespoon each of mango powder and garam masala
1 teaspoon red chilli powder	1 teaspoon red chili powder

1

Remove the stems, and wipe the aubergines (eggplants) with a damp cloth; slice them lengthways. Sprinkle the turmeric powder and 1 teaspoon sea salt over them; mix thoroughly, and let stand a few minutes.

2

Heat 2 tablespoons oil, and fry the aubergine (eggplant) slices until golden. Add garlic and ginger root, and fry another 2 minutes.

3

Add the remaining ingredients, one by one, together with the rest of the oil and more salt to taste and cook over medium heat 10 to 15 minutes.

4

Remove the pan from the heat and let it cool. Put the entire preparation in a clean, dry bottle or jar and put it out in the sun for 2 to 3 days.

5

Shake the container once or twice a day, and before each use. Serve as needed, and cover the container soon after each use.

CORNED MANGOES

(Chhile Aam ka Noncha)

Serves	*30 helpings or more*
Preparation time	*15 minutes plus maturing time*

This pickle has a haunting taste, and it must be the easiest to make! It is sure to inject life into the blandest of meals; one piece of the pickled mango is usually sufficient per person, per meal. It is very suitable for picnics and parties, too. Adjust the quantity of salt and asafoetida to your liking.

Imperial (Metric)	*American*
2 lb (900g) green mangoes	2 pounds green mangoes
1 teaspoon asafoetida powder	1 teaspoon asafoetida powder
1 teaspoon red chilli powder	1 teaspoon red chili powder
Large pinch of cumin powder	Large dash of cumin powder
2 tablespoons sea salt (or to taste)	2 tablespoons sea salt (or to taste)

1

Clean and wash the mangoes; peel and cut into 4 or 8 pieces each, according to their size.

2

Place the mangoes in a large bowl or on a platter. Add the rest of the ingredients, one by one, and blend thoroughly.

3

Take a dry and sterilized lidded glass jar and put the spiced mango pieces in it; sprinkle on some more salt if desired. Place the jar out in the sun, covering the mouth, for about a week. Do not forget to bring the jar indoors at night.

4

When the pickle matures — becomes a little sticky — and all the ingredients are well blended, serve as needed.

5

Shake the jar once a day, during maturity and after, and close the lid after each use.

PICKLED LEMON

(Neebu ka Achaar)

Serves	*20 helpings or more*
Preparation time	*15 minutes plus maturing time*

The Indian lemons with paper-thin skins (kaagazi neebu) are the best suited for this pickle; failing that, find the thinnest-skinned lemons you can — the Indian lemons are not much bigger than a ping-pong ball. The amount of salt and lemon juice can be adjusted to your liking. This lasts up to a month provided you have made enough!

Imperial (Metric)	*American*
1 lb (450g) juicy lemons	1 pound juicy lemons
½ lb (225g) sea salt	¾ cup sea salt
2 tablespoons carom seeds	2 tablespoons carom seeds
Large pinch of asafoetida powder	Large dash of asafoetida powder
2 teaspoons red chilli powder	2 teaspoons red chili powder
½ pint (300ml) lemon juice	1¼ cups lemon juice

1

Wipe the lemons thoroughly with a damp cloth; then cut them into four, leaving them whole at the bottom. Remove the pips.

2

Saving 2 tablespoons salt for later on, mix the remaining salt with the carom seeds, and asafoetida and chilli powders; stuff this mixture into the lemons, still keeping them whole (rather like flowers).

3

Take a clean, dry, sterilized crock, and sprinkle the reserved salt at its base. Then position the lemons in the crock. Any surplus spice mixture should be dropped on top of the lemons.

4

Pour in the lemon juice, cover the crock's mouth with a clean cloth, and put it out in the sun (bringing it in during the nights) for 7 to 10 days, or until the lemon skin is soft and the lemons are darker in colour.

5

Shake the crock at least once a day, and cover the crock after each use. Usually one-quarter of a lemon is plenty per person, per meal.

NOTE: The lemon juice can be heated before being added to the lemons in order to save on the maturing time.

STUFFED RED CHILLIES

(Bharwaan Laal Mirch)

Serves	20 helpings or more
Preparation time	15 minutes plus maturing time

Use fresh, plump chillies whose skin has turned red for this pickle; the green variety may also be used as a last resort. The filling mixture can be bound by oil or vinegar instead of lemon juice. Similarly, the final lubrication of the pickle can be done with lemon juice or vinegar instead of oil. A very useful pickle to have around; serve with meals or snacks.

Imperial (Metric)	American
1 lb (450g) fresh red chillies	1 pound fresh red chilies
2 oz (50g) each of coriander, mustard, cumin seeds and fennel	½ cup each of coriander, mustard, cumin seeds and fennel
1 teaspoon fenugreek seeds	1 teaspoon fenugreek seeds
1 teaspoon turmeric powder	1 teaspoon turmeric powder
2 oz (50g) mango powder (amchoor)	½ cup mango powder (amchoor)
2 tablespoons sea salt (or to taste)	2 tablespoons sea salt (or to taste)
3 tablespoons lemon juice	¼ cup lemon juice
1 pint (600ml) mustard oil	2½ cups mustard oil

1

Wash and dry the chillies; slit them lengthways, and carefully scoop out the inside. Do not halve the chillies, and keep their stems intact.

2

Dry roast the next 5 items — from coriander to sea salt — and grind them together. Add the chilli flesh and mix thoroughly. Heat the lemon juice, and pour in the ground mixture to bind. Stuff the chillies with this mixture.

3

Place the stuffed chillies inside a dry, sterilized glass jar. Heat the oil and, when a little cool, pour it over the chillies.

4

Cover the jar with a lid or clean cloth, and put it out in the sun for a week, or until the chilli skins assume a deeper colour. Shake the jar at least once a day.

5

Serve when needed, and cover the jar after each use.

PICKLED GOOSEBERRIES

(Karonde ka Achaar)

Serves   20 helpings or more

Preparation time   15 minutes plus soaking and maturing time

This pickle can also be made with blackberries (phaalse) or cape gooseberries (rasbhari) instead of gooseberries (karonde), or with oil or vinegar instead of lemon juice. A delightful sour pickle which truly completes a meal.

Imperial (Metric)	American
1 lb (450g) gooseberries	1 pound gooseberries
Sea salt to taste	Sea salt to taste
½ teaspoon turmeric powder	½ teaspoon turmeric powder
1 teaspoon cayenne	1 teaspoon cayenne
1 teaspoon each of cumin and mustard seeds, coarsely ground	1 teaspoon each of cumin and mustard seeds, coarsely ground
Pinch of asafoetida powder	Dash of asafoetida powder
½ pint (300ml) lemon juice	1¼ cups lemon juice

1

Clean and soak the gooseberries in water for 2 hours. Drain off the water; cut the gooseberries in half, and remove the pips.

2

Put the gooseberries in a clean and dry glass jar with a lid. Add the remaining ingredients, except the lemon juice, one by one. Shake the jar thoroughly to blend the ingredients.

3

Pour in the lemon juice, cover with the lid, and put the jar out in the sun for about a week, taking it indoors during the night. Alternatively, place the jar in the warmest place in the house (it will take longer to mature). You may heat up the lemon juice before adding it to the gooseberries in order to save on maturing time.

4

Serve as needed. Store in a warm place, and shake the jar at least once a day. Cover with the lid after each use.

BITTERGOURD PICKLE

(Karele ka Achaar)

Serves   15 helpings or more

Preparation time   20 minutes plus par boiling and maturing time

Bittergourds are now readily available even in the supermarkets of the West. Once the bitterness of the gourds is gone, the pickle cannot but please the lovers of variety. Half of one pickled bittergourd is usually sufficient per person, per meal.

Imperial (Metric)	American
10 small, fresh bittergourds	10 small, fresh bittergourds
Sea salt as needed	Sea salt as needed
2 tablespoons coriander seeds	2 tablespoons coriander seeds
1 tablespoon white cumin seeds	1 tablespoon white cumin seeds
1 tablespoon carom seeds	1 tablespoon carom seeds
½ teaspoon whole black peppercorns	½ teaspoon whole black peppercorns
5 cloves	5 cloves
1 tablespoon black cardamom seeds	1 tablespoon black cardamom seeds
1 tablespoon mustard seeds	1 tablespoon mustard seeds
1 tablespoon mango powder (amchoor)	1 tablespoon mango powder (amchoor)
Pinch of asafoetida powder	Dash of asafoetida powder
½ pint (300ml) mustard oil	1¼ cups mustard oil

1

Clean and wash the bittergourds; thickly peel their outer skins (do not discard the skin), and slit them lengthways without halving them. Parboil them, and the skins, in water; drain off the water and squeeze the gourds and the skins dry, then sprinkle 1 tablespoon sea salt over them.

2

Dry roast the next 7 ingredients — from coriander seeds to mustard seeds — in a frying pan for 2 to 3 minutes. Then grind them coarsely. Mix the mango and asafoetida powders. Add 2 tablespoons oil and the gourd skins, and blend the mixture thoroughly.

3

Stuff the mixture into the bittergourds, and arrange them in a clean crock. Spread the remaining spice mixture over them. Pour in the oil, and add more salt as required. Cover the mouth of the crock with a clean cloth, and put the crock out in the sun for a week or so.

4

To save on maturing time, heat the oil before adding it to the pickle. The gourds will become darker in colour, and the oil will become dark golden to denote that the pickle is ready to serve as needed.

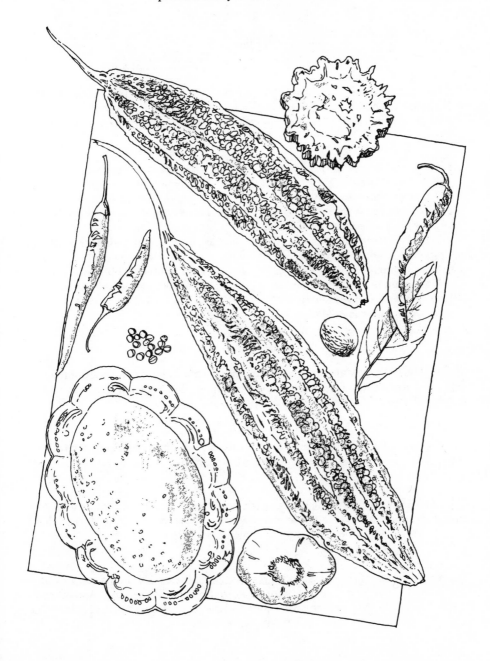

BLACK GRAMS PICKLE

(Chane ka Achaar)

Serves   20 helpings or more
Preparation time   20 minutes plus soaking and maturing time

Here is a novelty, and one that will please pickle lovers no end. This pickle should ideally be made with the dark grams available from your Indian grocer, but it can be made with chick peas as well. Feel free to use vinegar or lemon juice instead of oil.

Imperial (Metric)	American
1 lb (450g) dark brown grams or chick peas	2 cups garbanzo beans
1 teaspoon turmeric powder	1 teaspoon turmeric powder
Sea salt to taste	Sea salt to taste
1 teaspoon each of fenugreek seeds and fennel	1 teaspoon each of fenugreek seeds and fennel
1 tablespoon each of coriander seeds and mango powder	1 tablespoon each of coriander seeds and mango powder
1 teaspoon red chilli powder	1 teaspoon red chili powder
Large pinch of asafoetida powder	Large dash of asafoetida powder
Mustard oil as needed	Mustard oil as needed

1

Soak the beans in water to cover overnight. Drain off the water; pick out the unsoaked beans and discard them. Add the turmeric and 1 teaspoon salt, and mix well; then let dry in a cool place.

2

Dry roast all the items listed after salt, to chilli powder, in a hot frying pan for 2 minutes; then grind coarsely.

3

Sprinkle the asafoetida at the base of a dry and sterilized bottle or jar and add the beans and ground spices together with any additional salt to taste. Pour in enough oil to submerge the contents completely.

4

Cover the mouth of the container with a cloth, and leave it out in the sun 7 to 10 days. Shake the bottle/jar once or twice a day, and before each serving. Add more oil if necessary. When the beans change colour and the oil becomes dark and golden, the pickle is ready. Serve as needed.

ONION PICKLE

(Pyaaz ka Achaar)

Serves   10 helpings or more
Preparation time   15 minutes plus drying and maturing time
Cooking time   20 minutes

This pickle has its own exotic taste and is nothing like its western cousin, the pickled onion, available in sealed bottles in the supermarket! It can be made with any vegetable oil. Button onions are best suited for this concoction.

Imperial (Metric)	American
1 lb (450g) button onions	1 pound button onions
1 teaspoon turmeric powder	1 teaspoon turmeric powder
Sea salt as needed	Sea salt as needed
1 tablespoon each of coriander and mustard seeds	1 tablespoon each of coriander and mustard seeds
1 teaspoon fenugreek seeds	1 teaspoon fenugreek seeds
2 teaspoons fennel	2 teaspoons fennel
1 teaspoon cayenne	1 teaspoon cayenne
½ pint (300ml) cider vinegar	1¼ cups cider vinegar

1

Peel the onions, and wipe with a damp cloth; sprinkle the turmeric powder and 1 teaspoon sea salt over them. Mix well, and leave overnight to soak.

2

Dry roast the next 4 items, from coriander to cayenne, in a frying pan for 5 minutes, then coarsely grind them.

3

Place the vinegar in a saucepan with the ground spices, and bring to a boil over moderate heat. Add the onions, together with any needed extra salt, and bring to a boil again. Remove pan from heat, cover with a lid, and let the contents cool.

4

Transfer the contents to a clean, dry crock; cover its mouth with a clean cloth and place it in the sun for about a week. Shake the crock at least once a day, and take it indoors every night, or when it rains.

5

Serve as needed, with a meal or snacks; cover the crock after each use.

PICKLED JACKFRUIT

(Kathal ka Achaar)

Serves	10 helpings or more
Preparation time	25 minutes plus maturing time
Cooking time	10 minutes

Jackfruit is available at Asian grocers in season. It is, alas, not as readily available as most other Indian vegetables. This pickle is usually made with oil; it can, of course, be made with lemon juice or vinegar instead. A delightful pickle that lasts a good couple of months if you have made sufficient quantities! Adjust the quantity of oil to your liking.

Imperial (Metric)	*American*
1 lb (450g) jackfruit pieces, ready weight	1 pound jackfruit pieces, ready weight
2 tablespoons each of coriander, mustard and anise seeds	2 tablespoons each of coriander, mustard and anise seeds
1 tablespoon each of nigella and fenugreek seeds	1 tablespoon each of nigella and fenugreek seeds
1 tablespoon each of turmeric and mango powders	1 tablespoon each of turmeric and mango powders
2 tablespoons sea salt (or to taste)	2 tablespoons sea salt (or to taste)
2 teaspoons cayenne	2 teaspoons cayenne
Mustard oil as necessary	Mustard oil as necessary
1 teaspoon asafoetida powder	1 teaspoon asafoetida powder

1

Place the jackfruit pieces in a saucepan, and boil in water until tender. Drain off the water, and squeeze the pieces dry.

2

Dry roast the next 5 items listed, from coriander to cayenne, in a frying pan for about 5 minutes; then grind coarsely together.

3

Add about 3 tablespoons oil to the ground spice mixture, and make a thick paste; smear this paste thickly over the jackfruit pieces.

4

Sprinkle the asafoetida at the base of a dry, sterilized jar of adequate size, then drop in the spiced jackfruit pieces. Pour in enough oil to submerge the jackfruit pieces.

5

Cover the jar, and put it out in the sun for 10 to 12 days. When the oil is soaked up by the jackfruit, add more. Shake the jar once or twice a day.

6

Serve as needed. Shake the jar before serving, and cover it after each use.

GREEN BEAN PICKLE

(Sem ka Achaar)

Serves	15 helpings or more
Preparation time	20 minutes plus maturing time
Cooking time	20 minutes

This is a pickle you can make with any long, green beans of your choice. You may also use other green vegetables like Indian marrow (squash) or lauki, courgette (zucchini) or torai, or cucumber — kheera or kakdi. Instead of oil; lemon juice or vinegar can be used. A delightful seasonal pickle; do not make it to last much longer than a fortnight.

Imperial (Metric)	American
1 lb (450g) green beans	1 pound green beans
1 teaspoon turmeric powder	1 teaspoon turmeric powder
Sea salt to taste	Sea salt to taste
10 black peppercorns	10 black peppercorns
1 tablespoon each of coriander, mustard and carom seeds	1 tablespoon each of coriander, mustard and carom seeds
1 teaspoon fenugreek seeds	1 teaspoon fenugreek seeds
1 tablespoon fennel	1 tablespoon fennel
2 teaspoons mango powder	2 teaspoons mango powder
Pinch of asafoetida powder	Dash of asafoetida powder
½ pint (300ml) vegetable oil	1¼ cups vegetable oil

1

Wash and dry the beans; trim and cut them into medium-sized pieces. Boil in water for about 10 minutes. Then drain off the water, and transfer the beans to a large bowl or plate.

2

Lightly dry roast the ingredients listed, from turmeric powder to mango powder, and grind them together but not too finely. Add the ground spices to the beans and mix thoroughly; then leave to dry off in the shade.

3

Sprinkle the asafoetida powder at the base of a clean, dry, and sterilized crock. Then drop in the spiced green beans.

4

Heat the oil, then let it cool. Pour it into the crock with the beans, cover the mouth of the crock with a muslin cloth, and put it out in the sun for 2 days. Serve as needed. Shake the crock before each use; do not leave it open for too long.

SWEET AND SWEET-AND-SOUR PICKLES

(Meethe aur Khatmitthe Achaar)

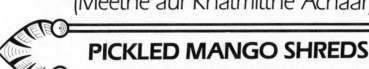

PICKLED MANGO SHREDS

(Aam ka Chhoonda)

Serves	*20 helpings or more*
Preparation time	*15 minutes plus maturing time*

This must be the easiest and quickest recipe around for a sweet mango pickle; it takes about a week to mature in the sun, slightly longer otherwise. Children love it; they start sampling it even before it is ready.

Imperial (Metric)	American
1 lb (450g) green mangoes	1 pound green mangoes
Sea salt to taste	Sea salt to taste
Pinch of asafoetida powder	Dash of asafoetida powder
1 teaspoon red chilli powder	1 teaspoon red chili powder
1 tablespoon each of cumin seeds and fennel, roasted and coarsely ground	1 tablespoon each of cumin seeds and fennel, roasted and coarsely ground
1 lb (450g) raw cane sugar	2 cups raw sugar

1

Wash, peel, and shred the mangoes; sprinkle on the salt and asafoetida, and blend thoroughly.

2

Place this mixture in a clean and dry crock or jar. Add the rest of the ingredients, one by one, and cover the crock with a clean muslin cloth.

3

Put the jar out in the sun for about a week; when the sugar has blended in with the rest of the ingredients in the shape of a golden, thick syrup, the pickle is ready. In the absence of sun, keep in the warmest place in the house — it will then take a little longer to mature.

4

Shake the jar at least once a day; cover after each use.

SWEET LEMON PEEL

(Neebu-Chhilke ka Meetha Achaar)

Serves   10 helpings

Preparation time   15 minutes plus maturing time

Use the thin-skinned variety of Indian lemon for this preparation; it matures best in direct sunshine. In the absence of sun, leave the pickle in the warmest place in the house; it will then take a bit longer to mature. An excellent side dish that can last several months.

Imperial (Metric)	American
10 thin-skinned lemons	10 thin-skinned lemons
Pinch of asafoetida powder	Dash of asafoetida powder
Sea salt to taste	Sea salt to taste
1 teaspoon red chilli powder	1 teaspoon red chili powder
½ teaspoon fenugreek seeds	½ teaspoon fenugreek seeds
1 tablespoon fennel	1 tablespoon fennel
4 cloves	4 cloves
1-inch (2½cm) piece cinnamon stick, broken into small pieces	1-inch piece cinnamon stick, broken into small pieces
½ lb (225g) jaggery (unrefined palm sugar) in small pieces	½ pound jaggery (unrefined palm sugar) in small pieces
½ pint (300ml) lemon juice	1¼ cups lemon juice
1 teaspoon garam masala	1 teaspoon garam masala

1

Thickly peel the outer skins of the lemons. Make sure the whole skin comes off as one circular peel, from one end to the other; discard the lemon flesh.

2

Sprinkle the asafoetida powder at the base of a clean, dry, and sterilized glass jar and position the lemon peels over it. Then add the rest of the ingredients, one by one, in the order of listing.

3

Cover the mouth of the jar with a muslin cloth, and put it out in the sun, removing it at night and putting it out again next morning (or whenever the sun comes out!).

4

In about a week's time, the syrup in the pickle will thicken and assume a golden colour. At that stage the jar can be covered with a normal glass lid instead of the cloth. Another 2 or 3 days in the sun, and the pickle will be ready to serve. Shake the jar at least once a day; cover after each use.

PICKLED SWEET LEMON

(Neebu ka Meetha Achaar)

Serves   20 helpings
Preparation time   10 minutes plus maturing time
Cooking time   20 minutes

Use the smallest possible lemons for this pickle; obtain the thin-skinned lemons of Indian variety from your grocer if you can. Because of the combination of cooking and sunning, this pickle matures more quickly and can last for several weeks or months, provided you make enough to go that far!

Imperial (Metric)	American
5 juicy lemons	5 juicy lemons
¼ pint (150ml) vegetable oil	⅔ cup vegetable oil
2 oz (50g) raw cane sugar	¼ cup raw sugar
Sea salt to taste	Sea salt to taste
Pinch of turmeric powder	Dash of turmeric powder
½ teaspoon red chilli powder	½ teaspoon red chili powder
4 cloves	4 cloves
1 teaspoon fennel	1 teaspoon fennel
Pinch of garam masala	Dash of garam masala

1

Wash, dry, and quarter the lemons (do not remove the outer skin); remove the pips.

2

Place the oil in a saucepan, and put it over moderate heat; after 2 minutes add the sugar, salt, and turmeric, and cook another 2 to 3 minutes while stirring.

3

Add the lemons together with all the remaining ingredients one by one. Lower the heat and cook 10 to 15 minutes, or until the oil separates. Remove pan from heat, and let cool.

4

Pour the cooked mixture into a suitable washed and dried crock or glass jar. Place the jar, uncovered, in the sun for 2 to 3 days, and the pickle will be ready; then cover the jar, and put it in a warm place.

5

Serve as needed; cover the jar after each use. Shake the container at least once a day.

SWEET AND SOUR CHILLI

(Khat-Mitthee Mirch)

Serves	*10 helpings or more*
Preparation time	*10 minutes*
Cooking time	*25 minutes*

This pickle made from green chillies is strangely sweet and sour! It is instant and requires no maturing time; you may serve it as soon as it is cooked. A tasty side dish which lasts a good few days.

Imperial (Metric)	American
1 lb (450g) fresh green chillies	1 pound fresh green chilies
1 tablespoon ghee	1 tablespoon ghee
½ teaspoon turmeric powder	½ teaspoon turmeric powder
Pinch of asafoetida powder	Dash of asafoetida powder
½ lb (225g) molasses	½ cup molasses
½ pint (300ml) water	1¼ cups water
1 tablespoon sliced root ginger	1 tablespoon sliced root ginger
4 cloves garlic, sliced	4 cloves garlic, sliced
1 teaspoon fennel	1 teaspoon fennel
Sea salt to taste	Sea salt to taste
6 tablespoons lemon juice	½ cup lemon juice
1 teaspoon garam masala	1 teaspoon garam masala

1
Wash, then thickly slice the chillies.

2
Heat the ghee in a saucepan, and sauté the turmeric and asafoetida in it for 2 minutes; then add the molasses and water and bring to a boil.

3
Drop in the chillies together with the rest of the ingredients, one by one; lower heat, and cook another 10 to 15 minutes, or until the water evaporates and the pickle assumes the desired consistency.

4
Remove from heat, and let mixture cool. Serve as needed, storing the left-overs in a lidded jar for later use. Cover after each use.

SWEET TOMATO PICKLE

(Tamaatar ka Meetha Achaar)

Serves	*15 helpings or more*
Preparation time	*15 minutes*
Cooking time	*25 minutes*

This recipe will produce a truly exotic tomato pickle which you are unlikely to have tasted before. Delight your friends and family with your dexterity at pickle-making. You may make enough for a few weeks, but it won't keep much longer.

Imperial (Metric)	*American*
1 lb (450g) red tomatoes	1 pound red tomatoes
Sea salt to taste	Sea salt to taste
4 oz (100g) raw cane sugar	½ cup raw sugar
½ pint (300ml) water	1¼ cups water
1 teaspoon sliced, fresh ginger	1 teaspoon sliced, fresh ginger
1 tablespoon sliced, dried dates	1 tablespoon sliced, dried dates
Pinch each of nigella, cumin seeds and coriander seeds, all crushed	Dash each of nigella, cumin seeds and coriander seeds, all crushed
Pinch of cinnamon powder	Pinch of cinnamon powder
1 teaspoon red chilli powder	1 teaspoon red chili powder

1

Chop up the tomatoes, and place them in a saucepan with salt, sugar, and the measured water; put it over moderate heat, and bring to the boil.

2

Add the rest of the ingredients, one by one — in order of listing; lower the heat, and continue to cook until the mixture thickens — about 15 minutes.

3

Remove pan from heat, and let the pickle cool.

4

Serve as needed. Store the remainder in a suitable container for later use.

SWEET PICKLED GINGER

(Adrak ka Meetha Achaar)

Serves	20 helpings or more
Preparation time	20 minutes plus maturing time

You might not associate fresh root ginger with a delightful pickle; make this particular concoction and you will change your mind! It will last a couple of months and is good for health.

Imperial (Metric)	American
1 lb (450g) fresh ginger	1 pound green ginger
Sea salt to taste	Sea salt to taste
½ lb (225g) raw cane sugar	1 cup raw sugar
Pinch of asafoetida powder	Dash of asafoetida powder
1 pint (600ml) lemon juice	2½ cups lemon juice
2 tablespoons chopped, dry dates and sultanas	2 tablespoons chopped, dried dates and golden raisins
1 teaspoon each of red chilli and coriander powders, and garam masala	1 teaspoon each of red chili and coriander powders, and garam masala

1

Wash and dry the ginger; scrape its outer skin off, and grate the root into a bowl. Stir in sufficient salt (bearing in mind the sugar and lemon juice to be added), and then add sugar.

2

In a dry and sterilized glass jar, sprinkle the asafoetida powder at the base. Then add the salted and sugared ginger, and shake thoroughly.

3

Pour the lemon juice over the mixture, add the dates and sultanas (raisins) and blend well.

4

Sprinkle the red chilli and coriander powders together with garam masala on the preparation, cover the jar, and put it out in the sun about two weeks (failing the sun, keep the jar in the warmest place in the house for a bit longer).

5

Shake the jar once a day. Taste a little from time to time when you think the pickle is ready for you, but wait until it *is* ready. Serve as needed, and close the lid after each use.

PICKLED SWEET SULTANAS (RAISINS)

(Kishmish ka Meetha Achaar)

Serves	*10 helpings or more*
Preparation time	*15 minutes*
Cooking time	*30 minutes*

Sultanas (golden raisins) are sweet anyway, but this pickle will give you an exotic sweetness you never knew existed! It is quite suitable as a side dish like any other pickle. Instead of vinegar, this pickle can also be made with lemon or tamarind juice. Make more to last longer!

Imperial (Metric)	*American*
1 pint (600ml) cider vinegar	2½ cups cider vinegar
4 oz (100g) sultanas	⅔ cup golden raisins
1 oz (25g) sliced root ginger	1 ounce sliced ginger root
2 oz (50g) raw cane sugar	¼ cup raw sugar
½ teaspoon each of coarsely ground cumin and black cardamom seeds	½ teaspoon each of coarsely ground cumin and black cardamom seeds
2 teaspoons sea salt (or to taste)	2 teaspoons sea salt (or to taste)
½ teaspoon red chilli powder	½ teaspoon red chili powder

1

Place the vinegar in a suitable saucepan; put it over medium heat, and bring to the boil.

2

Keeping the saucepan on the heat, add the washed and dried sultanas (raisins) as well as the ginger and sugar. Cook until the vinegar is reduced by half — about 15 minutes.

3

Then stir in the remaining ingredients, one by one, and cook another 10 minutes or so, or until all the ingredients are well blended.

4

Remove the saucepan from the heat and let it cool; then store in a lidded jar or crock and serve when needed.

SWEET CAULIFLOWER

(Meetha Gobhi Achaar)

Serves	*10 helpings or more*
Preparation time	*15 minutes plus maturing time*
Cooking time	*20 minutes*

This delightful pickle can also be made with vinegar or tamarind juice, and instead of cauliflower you may use potato or turnip. The pickle tastes exotic and refreshing any way.

Imperial (Metric)	*American*
1 lb (450g) cauliflower florets	1 pound cauliflower florets
2 tablespoons chopped onion	2 tablespoons chopped onion
4 cloves garlic, sliced	4 cloves garlic, sliced
1 tablespoon sliced root ginger	1 tablespoon sliced ginger root
1 teaspoon turmeric powder	1 teaspoon turmeric powder
1 teaspoon coarsely ground coriander and cumin seeds	1 teaspoon coarsely ground coriander and cumin seeds
Large pinch of nigella	Large dash of nigella
2 teaspoons sea salt (or to taste)	2 teaspoons sea salt (or to taste)
½ pint (300ml) lemon juice	1¼ cups lemon juice
½ lb (225g) raw cane sugar	1 cup raw sugar
½ pint (300ml) water	1¼ cups water

1

Place the cauliflower, onion, garlic, and ginger in a saucepan and boil once in water; drain off the water.

2

When almost dry, put the vegetables in a deep bowl. Stir in the next 4 ingredients, from turmeric to salt, and blend thoroughly.

3

Drop the spiced vegetables into a dry, sterilized crock or glass jar of proper size. Pour in the lemon juice, cover the mouth of the jar with a muslin cloth, and leave it out in the sun for about a week (bringing the jar inside during the night).

4

Place the sugar and the measured water in a saucepan and give it two slow boils. Add to the pickle, which should now have been out in the sun for about a week.

5

Cover the crock again, and put it out in the sun for another week (or in the warmest place in the house, in which case it will take a little longer). When the juice becomes golden and thick, the pickle is ready.

6

Serve as needed. Shake the crock at least once a day; cover after each use.

SWEET MANGO SLICES

(Meethi Aam ki Phaanken)

Serves	*10 helpings or more*
Preparation time	*15 minutes*
Cooking time	*30 minutes*

I have been partial to this sweet pickle since my childhood; you should like it too. It is simple to make and tastes absolutely out of this world! Serve as a side dish with a meal, or use it for picnics and parties, too. Do not make more than to last two weeks.

Imperial (Metric)	*American*
6 green mangoes, medium size	6 green mangoes, medium size
1½ lb (675g) raw cane sugar	3 cups raw sugar
1½ pints (900ml) water	3¾ cups water
1 teaspoon sea salt	1 teaspoon sea salt
½ teaspoon freshly ground black pepper	½ teaspoon freshly ground black pepper
1 teaspoon nigella	1 teaspoon nigella
1 tablespoon coriander powder	1 tablespoon coriander powder
Pinch of crushed saffron strands	Dash of crushed saffron strands

1

Wash and peel the mangoes; cut into thin slices.

2

Place the sugar and measured water in a saucepan; put over medium heat, and bring to a boil.

3

Add the mango slices, salt, pepper, nigella, and coriander; lower heat and cook until the water has evaporated and the mixture assumes a thick consistency — about 20 minutes.

4

Sprinkle on the crushed saffron, cover the pan, and remove it from the heat; let cool.

5

Store in a covered container, and serve as needed. Cover the container after each use.

SWEET VEGETABLE PICKLE

(Sabziyon ka Meetha Achaar)

Serves	10 helpings or more
Preparation time	15 minutes
Cooking time	35 minutes

This is a sweet pickle of the cooked variety. It lends itself to a lot of experimentation. If you use the vegetables that your family and friends like, it is bound to be a hit! Serve with a meal or take out on a picnic; the choice is yours.

Imperial (Metric)	American
1 lb (450g) mixed vegetables, pieces not too small	1 pound mixed vegetables, pieces not too small
2 tablespoons mustard oil	2 tablespoons mustard oil
Pinch of asafoetida powder	Dash of asafoetida powder
½ teaspoon turmeric powder	½ teaspon turmeric powder
1 tablespoon ground root ginger	1 tablespoon ground ginger root
1 teaspoon ground garlic	1 teaspoon ground garlic
4 oz (100g) raw cane sugar	½ cup raw sugar
½ pint (300ml) water	1¼ cups water
½ teaspoon each of cayenne and crushed black peppercorns	½ teaspoon each of cayenne and crushed black peppercorns
1 tablespoon mango powder (amchoor)	1 tablespoon mango powder (amchoor)
1 tablespoon garam masala	1 tablespoon garam masala

1

Wash, peel, and cut the vegetables into convenient pieces; then parboil in water. Drain off the water, and put the vegetables to one side.

2

Heat the oil in a saucepan, and sauté the asafoetida and turmeric in it for 2 minutes over moderate heat. Then add ginger and garlic and cook, stirring, until golden.

3

Add the sugar and water, and give the mixture two quick boils. Now toss in the vegetables, together with the rest of the ingredients, and cook until the oil separates — about 10 to 15 minutes.

4

Remove the saucepan from the heat and, when cool, store the pickle in a lidded container. Serve as and when needed, covering after each use.

STUFFED, DRIED DATES PICKLE

(Bharwaan Chhuhaare ka Achaar)

Serves   15 helpings or more
Preparation time   20 minutes plus maturing time
Cooking time   20 minutes

This pickle has been made in my family for generations. It is another pickle that can also be made with vinegar. This stylish side dish can easily last a couple of months, if you have made enough of it! It is fit for a feast at any time.

Imperial (Metric)	American
1 lb (450g) dry dates	1 pound dried dates
1 tablespoon ghee	1 tablespoon ghee
1 tablespoon grated, fresh ginger	1 tablespoon grated, fresh ginger
Pinch of green cardamom powder	Dash of green cardamom powder
1 teaspoon each of mango powder,	1 teaspoon each of mango powder,
cumin seeds, pistachios and sultanas	cumin seeds, pistachios and golden
½ teaspoon black peppercorns	raisins
2 teaspoons sea salt (or to taste)	½ teaspoon black peppercorns
½ lb (225g) raw cane sugar	2 teaspoons sea salt (or to taste)
1 pint (600ml) lemon juice	1 cup raw sugar
	2½ cups lemon juice

1

Place the dried dates and water to cover in a saucepan and give them two quick boils. Remove the pan from the heat, and drain off the water. Slit the dates in the middle, keeping them whole, then carefully remove and discard the stones from the dates without disturbing their shape.

2

Heat the ghee in a frying pan; sauté first the ginger and cardamom powder for 2 minutes over moderate heat, then add the mango powder, cumin, pistachios, sultanas (raisins), and peppercorns. Stir-fry for about 5 minutes. Remove from the heat, and give all the stir-fried ingredients a pounding, using a pestle and mortar. Make a coarse mixture.

3

Fill the dates with the mixture, tying each one with a thread or fine string. Neatly arrange them in a liddled glass jar. Sprinkle the salt and sugar over them, and pour on the lemon juice. Cover with the lid, and leave the jar out in the sun all day (bringing it inside during the night) for about two weeks.

4

When the dates change their appearance and the juice becomes golden and thick, the pickle is ready. Serve as needed, and shake the jar carefully at least once a day. Cover after each use.

SWEET TURNIPS AND GREEN BEANS

(Shaljum aur Sem ka Meetha Achaar)

Serves	*20 helpings or more*
Preparation time	*15 minutes plus maturing time*
Cooking time	*30 minutes*

This preparation combines the cooking and sunning processes to produce a stunning sweet pickle, which easily lasts several weeks. A delightful side dish capable of bringing even an insipid meal to life!

Imperial (Metric)	American
1 lb (450g) turnips	1 pound turnips
1 lb (450g) green beans	1 pound green beans
½ pint (300ml) mustard oil	1¼ cups mustard oil
2 teaspoons sea salt (or to taste)	2 teaspoons sea salt (or to taste)
1 teaspoon cayenne	1 teaspoon cayenne
1 tablespoon mustard seeds, ground	1 tablespoon mustard seeds, ground
1 teaspoon each of cinnamon and cumin powders	1 teaspoon each of cinnamon and cumin powders
¼ pint (150ml) cider vinegar	⅔ cup cider vinegar
½ lb (225g) molasses	⅔ cup molasses
½ pint (300ml) water	1¼ cups water

1

Wash, trim, peel, and cut the turnips and green beans into convenient-sized pieces. Place them in a saucepan with water, and quickly boil twice. Remove the pan from the heat, and drain off the water.

2

Place the cooked vegetables in a deep bowl; add the oil, salt, cayenne, mustard, and cinnamon and cumin powders and blend thoroughly.

3

Put the spiced mixture in a dry glass jar, or crock. Add the vinegar, cover the mouth of the jar with muslin, and put it out in the hot sun for 1 week (or the warmest place in the house, in which case it will take a while longer) until the mixture turns sour.

4

Then place the molasses and the measured water in a saucepan, and give it two strong boils over moderate heat. Add this sweet liquid to the jar, and put it out in the sun for another week; the pickle will then be ready. Serve as and when needed.

Chapter 7

Preserves
(Murabbay)

The people of India have an incredibly sweet tooth and to eat lots of sweets — under one pretext or another — is customary in that country. Besides, "sweetening the mouth" of a guest is the first prerequisite of Indian hospitality. Given that guests can drop in at any time, especially when shops may be closed and sweets may not be readily available, hosts had to find an amicable solution to this problem. They explored and stumbled on the preserve! Unlike ordinary sweets, preserves last a long time. They claim to be good for the brain, cool the mind, and strengthen the heart tissues. Little wonder that they command such universal popularity!

Preserves are made from fruits and vegetables. They require elaborate preparation and meticulous attention to detail. There are several distinct stages in making the preserve. In the main these are: (1) preparing the main ingredient, (2) boiling, (3) preparing the syrup, and (4) preserving.

1.   Preparing the main ingredient: First of all the fruit or vegetable should be washed and peeled as prescribed; large fruits and vegetables should be cut into convenient-sized pieces. Stones in some fruits can be left in when preserving them. The main ingredient should be pricked thoroughly (lightly in the case of delicate ones) with a fork, to enable it to soak up as much syrup as possible, but make sure that the shape of the fruit or vegetable remains intact. After pricking, the main ingredient should be soaked and washed in water as prescribed.

2.   Boiling: Boiling the main ingredient tenderizes the stiff outer skin and makes it more receptive to the syrup; some fruits or vegetables require more than one boil. They are left in the water for differing periods before they are taken out.

3.   Preparing the syrup: Syrup for the preserves is made with sugar and water either in advance or at the time of preserving. The suggested proportion of sugar and water varies according to choice — 2 pints (1.15 litres/5 cups) water to 1 pound (450g) sugar; ½ pint (300ml/1¼ cups) water to 1 pound (450g) sugar — but I suggest 1 pint (600ml/2½ cups) water to 1 pound (450g) sugar for preserve dishes. Consistency of the syrup is a matter of personal preference, but for preserves it should not be less than one-string density or the preserve will go mouldy before long. Equally, the syrup should not be thicker than two-string consistency or there will be danger of granulation.

4. Preserving: When the fruit or vegetable has been prepared and boiled, it is often cooked in syrup. If, for whatever reason, some main ingredient (possibly because it is too delicate) seems in danger of breaking up while cooking, remove the fruit (or vegetable) and go on to complete the making of syrup, then just immerse the main ingredient in it. This should avoid possible disappointment. In order to ensure that the preserve stays fresh for a long period, it should be stored in a clean and dry crock or glass jar, sterilized and airtight. The lid of the container should be wiped clean and replaced after each use, and it should not be left open for too long.

Adding lemon juice to the syrup gives a new dimension to the preserve and improves the flavour of the dish. Besides, the lemon juice extracts and removes the inner salts of the fruits and vegetables and enables the preserves to last that much longer. The addition of green cardamom powder, rose water, or kewra water (or essence) keeps the preserve smelling fresh and fragrant. When serving, decorate the preserves with edible silver or gold foils (available at Asian grocery shops); they make the dish look more fetching and claim to have their own cooling attributes.

There is a glittering array of Indian fruits and vegetables suitable for making preserves. The scope for experimentation with other fruits and vegetables is almost unlimited. A fair selection is offered here, ranging from preserves made out of the common and well-known vegetables and fruits to the exotic and not so readily available — like the potato at one end and the "aamla" fruit at the other. I do hope that you will enjoy not only the making, eating, and offering of the preserves given in this book but will also be encouraged to try out a few ideas of your own!

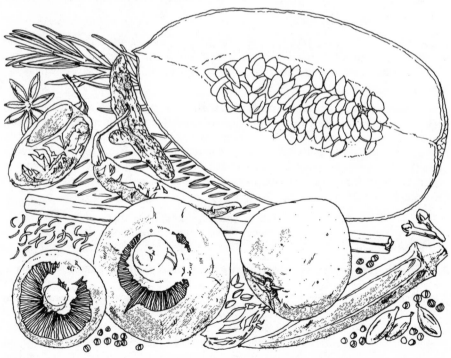

POTATO PRESERVE

(Aalu Murabba)

Serves	*10 helpings or more*
Preparation time	*20 minutes plus soaking time*
Cooking time	*35 minutes*

Some Indian homes make a rather large quantity of this preserve, to last a very long time. This dish not only serves as a delicious dessert, but it also enjoys the reputation of strengthening the heart muscle.

Imperial (Metric)	*American*
2 lb (900g) medium potatoes	2 pounds medium potatoes
1 teaspoon edible slaked lime	1 teaspoon edible slaked lime
Water as needed	Water as needed
2 lb (900g) raw cane sugar	4 cups raw sugar
2 teaspoons lemon juice	2 teaspoons lemon juice
1 teaspoon rose water	1 teaspoon rose water

1

Peel the potatoes, and prick them all over with a fork. Soak them in a mixture of lime and water about 2 hours. Then wash them in several changes of clean water, or thoroughly under cold, running water.

2

Place the potatoes in clean water in a deep saucepan; bring to the boil, and cook for 2 minutes. Then cover the pan, remove from heat, and allow to cool.

3

While the potatoes are boiling, in a separate saucepan make a one-string syrup with the sugar and water as needed. While the syrup is still on the stove, fish out the potatoes from the other saucepan and add to the syrup. Cook for about 5 minutes over a medium heat, or until the potatoes are tender and the syrup thickens.

4

Stir in the lemon juice, and soon afterwards remove the pan from the heat. Add the rose water before the mixture cools completely.

5

When cold, store the preserve in a sterilized dry crock or glass jar, and serve when needed.

CARROT PRESERVE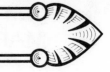

(Gaajar Murabba)

Serves	*10 helpings*
Preparation time	*20 minutes plus soaking time*
Cooking time	*40 minutes*

This delicious preserve soothes the heart and cools the mind. Serve cold in the morning, or whenever the mood takes you. A tantalizing sweet to dangle in front of children!

Imperial (Metric)	American
10 medium carrots	10 medium carrots
2 teaspoons sea salt	2 teaspoons sea salt
Water as needed	Water as needed
2 lb (900g) raw cane sugar	4 cups raw sugar
1 tablespoon lemon juice	1 tablespoon lemon juice
Pinch of crushed saffron strands	Dash of crushed saffron strands
1 teaspoon rose water	1 teaspoon rose water

1

Scrape the outer skin of the carrots, and prick them thoroughly but carefully. Sprinkle with the salt, and soak in water to cover about 30 minutes.

2

Wash the carrots in several changes of clean water; then drain off the water and put the carrots to one side.

3

In a saucepan boil enough water to submerge all the carrots. When the water comes to a boil, drop in the carrots, cover the pan, and remove from the heat; let cool.

4

Meanwhile, make a one-string syrup with the sugar and water as needed.

5

While the syrup is still on the stove, fish out the carrots from the water and drop into the syrup. Cook over moderate heat for about 10 minutes, until soft.

6

Stir in the lemon juice, and cook for another 2 minutes. Add the saffron and rose water, and remove the pan from the heat. Store in a clean, dry glass jar. Serve when needed.

MARROW (SQUASH) PRESERVE

(Lauki Murabba)

Serves	*10 helpings or more*
Preparation time	*15 minutes*
Cooking time	*30 minutes*

A novel preserve that has a cooling effect; very popular with the intellectual fraternity. Best served first thing in the morning, just before breakfast.

Imperial (Metric)	*American*
½ lb (225g) baby marrow	2 small baby squash
Large pinch of sea salt	Large dash of sea salt
1 lb (450g) raw cane sugar	2 cups raw sugar
Water as needed	Water as needed
Pinch of cardamom powder	Dash of cardamom powder
2 teaspoons lemon juice	2 teaspoons lemon juice
1 teaspoon kewra water	1 teaspoon kewra water

1

Peel the marrow (squash) and sprinkle its surface (all round) with salt. Leave for 5 minutes; then wash thoroughly and grate it.

2

Boil the grated marrow (squash) until soft; drain off the water, and put it on a plate for later use.

3

While the squash is boiling, take a large saucepan and, using sugar and water as necessary, make a one-string syrup.

4

While the syrup is still on the stove, add the marrow (squash) and continue cooking over moderate heat 5 to 7 minutes.

5

Sprinkle the cardamom powder over the cooking mixture; stir in the lemon juice, and cook another 2 minutes. Then remove the pan from the heat, sprinkle on the kewra, and let the preserve cool.

6

Store in a sterilized and airtight glass jar, and serve as and when needed.

WHITE RADISH PRESERVE

(Mooli Murabba)

Serves	*10 helpings or more*
Preparation time	*15 minutes plus soaking time*
Cooking time	*30 minutes*

This is a wholesome sweet dish to please that unexpected guest. Its cooling properties are clear from the beginning; the impact of the taste comes later!

Imperial (Metric)	*American*
2 lb (900g) white radish	2 pounds white radish
1 teaspoon sea salt	1 teaspoon sea salt
1 tablespoon edible lime powder	1 tablespoon edible lime powder
Water as needed	Water as needed
2 lb (900g) raw cane sugar	4 cups raw sugar
1 tablespoon lemon juice	1 tablespoon lemon juice
½ teaspoon cardamom powder	½ teaspoon cardamom powder
2 teaspoons kewra water	2 teaspoons kewra water

1

Wash the radish; scrape off the outer skin, chop off the tops and bottoms, and cut into pieces. Prick the pieces with a fork, and soak in a mixture of salt, lime, and water about two hours.

2

Wash the radish pieces in several changes of clean water, and then boil in water about 5 minutes. Remove the pan from the heat, drain the radish pieces, and let them dry.

3

In a separate saucepan, make a one-string syrup with the sugar and water as needed. While the syrup is still cooking, drop in the radish, and cook over low heat a further 5 minutes, or until the radish is tender.

4

Stir in the lemon juice, and cook a further 2 minutes. Then add the cardamom powder, and remove the pan from the heat.

5

Stir in the kewra water before the preparation gets cold. When cold, store the preserve in a dry crock, and serve when desired.

GREEN BANANA PRESERVE

(Kela Murabba)

Serves	*10 helpings or more*
Preparation time	*10 minutes*
Cooking time	*30 minutes*

Yet another delicious use of the banana; this proves its versatility! This preserve should be popular with the whole family. For variety, serve decorated with silver foils.

Imperial (Metric)	*American*
6 green bananas	6 green bananas
Water as needed	Water as needed
2 lb (900g) raw cane sugar	4 cups raw sugar
1 small juicy lemon	1 small juicy lemon
½ teaspoon green cardamom powder	½ teaspoon green cardamom powder
1 teaspoon kewra water	1 teaspoon kewra water

1
Wash the bananas; prick them all over the outer skin, and cut into large pieces.

2
In a saucepan, boil enough water and then drop in the banana pieces. Leave the pan over moderate heat another 2 minutes before removing it from the heat.

3
Take out the banana pieces, and remove the outer skin from each.

4
Make a one-string syrup with proportionate water and sugar. Squeeze in the lemon, and drop in the banana pieces. Remove the pan from the heat.

5
Add the cardamom powder while the concoction is cooling. Stir in the kewra water, and when the preserve is quite cold, store it in a sterilized crock.

6
Serve when needed.

APPLE PRESERVE

(Seb Murabba)

Serves 8 helpings	
Preparation time 25 minutes plus soaking time	
Cooking time 40 minutes	

Brainy people are partial to this famous preserve. It lasts a long time and is a must for all sophisticated Indian homes.

Imperial (Metric)	*American*
8 medium eating apples, firm	8 medium eating apples, firm
2 oz (50g) edible lime powder	2 ounces edible lime powder
Water as needed	Water as needed
2 lb (900g) raw cane sugar	2 pounds raw sugar
Pinch of cardamom powder	Dash of cardamom powder
4 drops kewra essence	4 drops kewra essence
Silver foils, to serve	Silver foils, to serve

1

Wash the apples, and then peel them. Keeping them whole, prick them all over with a fork.

2

Mix the eating lime and water to cover, and soak the apples in this mixture about 2 hours. Rinse the apples thoroughly in several changes of clean water, and then let them dry.

3

Place enough water to cover the apples in a deep saucepan, and bring it to the boil. Drop the apples in, cover the pan, and remove it from the heat; leave it to cool.

4

Make a one-string syrup with the sugar and water as necessary. Take the apples out of the water, and add to the syrup. Cook until the apples are soft and the syrup thickens.

5

Add the kewra essence to the mixture, remove the pan from the heat, and let it cool. Store in an airtight container.

6

Serve when needed, decorated with a foil.

MANGO PRESERVE

(Aam Murabba)

Serves	10 helpings or more
Preparation time	15 minutes plus soaking time
Cooking time	35 minutes

This is one of the premier preserves of India and is popular with the whole family!
Given its healthy and nutritious attributes, serve it cold at any time of the day or
night!

Imperial (Metric)	American
2 lb (900g) small, green mangoes	2 pounds small, green mangoes
1 tablespoon edible slaked lime	1 tablespoon edible slaked lime
Water as needed	Water as needed
2 lb (900g) raw cane sugar	4 cups raw sugar
1 tablespoon lemon juice	1 tablespoon lemon juice
Pinch of crushed saffron strands	Dash of crushed saffron strands
1 teaspoon kewra water	1 teaspoon kewra water
Edible gold foil, to serve	Edible gold foil, to serve

1

Peel the mangoes, and prick them thoroughly. Mix the lime with enough water, and
soak the mangoes in this for about an hour.

2

Wash the mangoes in several changes of clean water; then place them in a saucepan
with water to cover, and bring the water to the boil. Remove the pan from the heat,
and allow to cool.

3

Meanwhile, make a one-string syrup with the sugar and water as needed. While the
syrup is boiling, add the mangoes to the syrup. Cook over medium heat for another
10 minutes, or until the mangoes are tender and the syrup thickens.

4

Stir in the lemon juice, and remove the pan from the heat. Add the saffron while the
preparation is cooling of.

5

Add the kewra water when the preserve is cold; store the preserve in a dry, airtight
crock, and serve when needed. Decorate each serving with a foil.

PAPAYA PRESERVE

(Papeeta Murabba)

Serves	*10 helpings or more*
Preparation time	*20 minutes plus soaking time*
Cooking time	*40 minutes*

Not a commonly known preserve, but nevertheless no less delicious for it. Serve in the morning, or after meals; it will win you over either way!

Imperial (Metric)	American
4 medium, green papayas	4 medium, green papayas
1 teaspoon sea salt	1 teaspoon sea salt
Water as needed	Water as needed
2 lbs (900g) raw cane sugar	4 cups raw sugar
Pinch of cardamom powder	Dash of cardamom powder
1 teaspoon kewra water	1 teaspoon kewra water
Silver foils, to serve	Silver foils, to serve

1

Peel the papayas, remove the seeds, and cut the flesh into convenient-sized pieces. Prick the pieces carefully, and soak them in a mixture of salt and water about 30 minutes. Then wash with clean water.

2

Boil enough water in a deep saucepan; drop in the papaya pieces, and continue to cook over medium heat about 5 minutes. Remove the pan from the heat, and allow to cool.

3

Make a one-string syrup with the sugar and water as needed. While the syrup is still cooking, drop the papaya pieces into it, and cook until the papaya is tender and the syrup thickens.

4

Sprinkle the cardamom powder over the preparation, and remove the pan from the heat. Stir in the kewra water before the mixture is cold.

5

When cold, store the preserve in a clean, dry, airtight glass jar and serve when needed, each serving decorated with a silver foil.

BLACKBERRY PRESERVE

(Phaalsa Murabba)

Serves   20 helpings or more

Preparation time   10 minutes plus drying and melting times

Cooking time   30 minutes

A pre-breakfast delicacy of its own ilk; feel free to serve it as dessert or whenever the mood strikes you. The dish is known for its cooling and revitalizing properties.

Imperial (Metric)	American
2 lb (900g) blackberries	2 pounds blackberries
Water as needed	Water as needed
Large pinch of sea salt	Large dash of sea salt
2 lb (900g) raw cane sugar	4 cups raw sugar
1 tablespoon lemon juice	1 tablespoon lemon juice
Large pinch of green cardamom powder	Large dash of green cardamom powder
6 drops kewra essence	6 drops kewra essence
Edible silver foil, to serve	Edible silver foil, to serve

1

Wash the blackberries. Boil enough water to cover, with the salt, in a saucepan. Drop in the blackberries, remove the pan from the heat, and allow to cool.

2

Drain the blackberries and wash them, carefully, with clean water. Take them out and let them dry.

3

Place the blackberries in a saucepan, cover with half the sugar, and leave for 6 to 8 hours.

4

In a separate saucepan make a one-string syrup with the remaining sugar and enough water. While the syrup is still cooking, add the blackberries covered with sugar; cook another 10 minutes over low heat. Stir carefully, add the lemon juice, and remove the pan from the heat.

5

Add the cardamom powder and kewra — in that order — before the preparation cools off. When cold, store the preserve in a suitable container, which should be airtight and sterilized.

6

Serve when needed; decorate each serving with a silver foil.

APRICOT PRESERVE

(Khubaani Murabba)

Serves	*10 helpings or more*
Preparation time	*5 minutes*
Cooking time	*30 minutes*

A dainty preserve to keep the children quiet; it also makes your dining table look attractive. Leave the stones in the apricots, but don't eat them when the preserve is served. They will look like shining gold bulbs!

Imperial (Metric)	American
2 lb (900g) fresh, firm apricots	2 pounds fresh, firm apricots
Water as needed	Water as needed
2 lb (900g) raw cane sugar	4 cups raw sugar
1 tablespoon lemon juice	1 tablespoon lemon juice
1 teaspoon rose water	1 teaspoon rose water
Edible gold foils, to serve	Edible gold foils, to serve

1

Prick the apricots lightly but carefully; then wash well.

2

Make a one-string syrup with water and sugar. While the syrup is still on the stove, drop in the apricots and cook over medium heat for about 10 minutes.

3

Stir in the lemon juice, lower the heat, and cook a further 5 minutes. Remove the pan from the heat, and leave it to cool.

4

Add the rose water before the preparation cools off. When cold, store the preserve in a suitable airtight container, and serve when needed. Decorate each serving with a foil.

ORANGE PRESERVE

(Naarangi Murabba)

Serves 8

Preparation time   15 minutes plus soaking time

Cooking time   40 minutes

This preparation can prove to be a popular dessert, especially in those households where the members are fond of sweets and there is no shop open!

Imperial (Metric)	*American*
8 small, firm oranges	8 small, firm oranges
1 teaspoon edible slaked lime	1 teaspoon edible slaked lime
1 teaspoon powdered chalk	1 teaspoon powdered chalk
Water as needed	Water as needed
2 lb (900g) raw cane sugar	4 cups raw sugar
Pinch of crushed saffron strands	Dash of crushed saffron strands
1 teaspoon rose water	1 teaspoon rose water

1

Wash the oranges, and prick them all over with a fork. Cover them with the lime and chalk, and soak in water for about 2 hours.

2

Wash the oranges in several changes of clean water; then put them in fresh water, and boil about 5 minutes. Remove the pan from the heat, and let cool.

3

Make a one-string syrup with the sugar and water as needed. While the syrup is still on the stove, take out the oranges, and drop them in the syrup. When the oranges are cooked and the syrup thickens, remove the pan from the heat.

4

Stir the saffron and rose water into the concoction while it cools. When cold, store in a sterilized and airtight crock or glass jar. Serve when needed.

PEAR PRESERVE

(Naashpaati Murabba)

Serves   8 helpings
Preparation time   20 minutes plus soaking time
Cooking time   35 minutes

This preserve is a popular confection with everyone. It has remarkable cooling properties and enables you to keep a cool head.

Imperial (Metric)	American
8 medium, firm pears	8 medium, firm pears
1 teaspoon sea salt	1 teaspoon sea salt
Water as needed	Water as needed
2 lb (900g) raw cane sugar	4 cups raw sugar
2 teaspoons lemon juice	2 teaspoons lemon juice
Pinch of cardamom powder	Dash of cardamom powder
1 teaspoon kewra water	1 teaspoon kewra water

1

Wash and peel the pears, and prick them all over. Make a mixture of salt and water, and soak the pears in it for about 2 hours. Then wash the pears thoroughly with cold, clean water.

2

Boil enough water in a deep saucepan to cover; drop the pears in while it is boiling. Cover the pan, remove it from the heat, and let cool.

3

Make a one-string syrup with the sugar and water as needed. Take the pears from the water, and add them to the syrup while it is still on the stove. Cook another 10 minutes, or until the pears are tender and the syrup begins to thicken. Stir in the lemon juice, and remove the pan from the heat.

4

Sprinkle in the cardamom powder, and sprinkle the kewra water over the mixture before it cools.

5

When cool, store the preserve in a sterilized and dry crock or glass jar. Serve when needed.

GRAPE PRESERVE

(Angoor Murabba)

Serves	10 helpings or more
Preparation time	10 minutes
Cooking time	30 minutes

A delicious preserve, which is good for the brain, and lasts a long time.

Imperial (Metric)	American
½ lb (225g) black grapes	1 cup black grapes
1 lb (450g) raw cane sugar	2 cups raw sugar
Water as needed	Water as needed
8 strands of saffron, crushed	8 strands of saffron, crushed
1 teaspoon rose water	1 teaspoon rose water
Silver foils, to serve	Silver foils, to serve

1

Wash the grapes thoroughly, but carefully, in two changes of water.

2

In a deep saucepan, use sugar and water as needed to make a one-string syrup.

3

Add the grapes to the syrup, and cook over medium heat a further 5 minutes. Sprinkle the saffron over the preparation; remove the pan from the heat, and let it cool.

4

Sprinkle the rose water over the preserve, turn over carefully, and store in a clean, dry, and airtight container. Serve when needed, decorated with a silver foil.

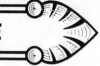

GOOSEBERRY PRESERVE

(Rasbhari Murabba)

Serves	*10 helpings or more*
Preparation time	*10 minutes*
Cooking time	*40 minutes*

Use the original Indian "rashbaris" (cape gooseberries) for this preparation; these pretty fruits are golden berries encased in loose papery balloons something like Chinese lanterns. The preserve made from these is as salubrious as it is exquisite.

Imperial (Metric)	American
1 lb (450g) golden gooseberries	1 pound golden gooseberries
Pinch of sea salt	Dash of sea salt
Water as needed	Water as needed
1 lb (450g) raw cane sugar	2 cups raw sugar
1 teaspoon lemon juice	1 teaspoon lemon juice
Pinch of crushed saffron strands	Dash of crushed saffron strands
2 teaspoons rose water	2 teaspoons rose water

1

Peel off the outer skins and remove stems from the gooseberries; then wash with care.

2

Add the salt to enough water in a saucepan to cover, and bring to a boil. Place the whole gooseberries in a porous cloth, make a loose bundle, and dip in the boiling water two or three times. Then take them out, and place on a plate.

3

Make a one-string syrup with sugar and water as needed. While the syrup is still on the stove, drop in the gooseberries, and cook until the gooseberries are tender (but not broken) and the syrup thickens.

4

Stir in the lemon juice, and add the saffron to the mixture; remove the pan from the heat, and leave to cool.

5

Add the rose water to the preserve before it cools completely. When cold, store the preparation in a sterilized glass jar; serve when needed.

GUAVA PRESERVE

(Amrood Murabba)

Serves	*10 helpings or more*
Preparation time	*15 minutes plus soaking time*
Cooking time	*45 minutes*

An exotic although slightly unusual preserve. It has a delightful taste and possesses wholesome and sustaining properties. Serve before breakfast or as a dessert.

Imperial (Metric)	American
2 lb (900g) firm guavas	2 pounds firm guavas
2 tablespoons edible slaked lime	2 tablespoons edible slaked lime
1 teaspoon sea salt	1 teaspoon sea salt
Water as needed	Water as needed
2 lb (900g) raw cane sugar	4 cups raw sugar
1 tablespoon lemon juice	1 tablespoon lemon juice
½ teaspoon cardamom powder	½ teaspoon cardamom powder
Edible silver foils, to serve	Edible silver foils, to serve

1

Wash the guavas, and prick them carefully with a fork. Make a mixture of lime, salt, and water, and soak the guavas in it for 2 hours.

2

Wash the guavas in several changes of clean water; then boil them in fresh water. Remove the pan from the heat, and take the guavas out.

3

Make a one-string syrup with sugar and water as needed. While the syrup is still on the stove, add the guavas, and cook for another 10 minutes over a moderate heat, or until the guavas are tender and the syrup thickens.

4

Stir in the lemon juice, cover the pan, and cook another 5 minutes. Remove the pan from the heat, add the cardamom powder, and allow to cool.

5

When cold, store the preserve in a clean, dry, and airtight crock; serve when needed. Decorate each serving with a foil.

PINEAPPLE PRESERVE

(Anannas Murabba)

Serves	10 helpings or more
Preparation time	20 minutes plus dripping and melting time
Cooking time	30 minutes

This preserve boosts the brain and cools the mind. It is a handy confection to have around the house; feel free to serve it either first thing in the morning or after meals.

Imperial (Metric)	American
2 lb (900g) pineapple, ready weight	2 pounds pineapple, ready weight
1 tablespoon edible slaked lime	1 tablespoon edible slaked lime
Water as needed	Water as needed
2 lb (900g) raw cane sugar	4 cups raw sugar
1 tablespoon lemon juice	1 tablespoon lemon juice
Pinch of cardamom powder	Dash of cardamom powder
1 teaspoon kewra water	1 teaspoon kewra water

1

Cut the pineapple into big pieces; prick the pieces all over — taking care not to break them — and smear them with the lime and a little extra water. Place the pieces on a porous cloth, and make a bundle. Hang up for about 2 hours so that the excess moisture drips away.

2

Take out the pineapple pieces, wash thoroughly, and boil for about 5 minutes.

3

Spread about ½ lb (225g/1 cup) sugar at the base of a large, lidded pan. Arrange the pineapple pieces over the sugar, and pour another ½ lb (225g/1 cup) sugar over the pineapple. Cover the pan, and leave overnight.

4

By the next morning the sugar will have melted into syrup and will have penetrated into the pineapple pieces. Place the pan over moderate heat, and bring to a boil. Add the remaining sugar, and cook until the syrup is of at least one-string consistency and the pineapple is tender.

5

Stir in the lemon juice, and cook a further 5 minutes. Then sprinkle the cardamom powder over the preparation, and remove the pan from the heat.

Add the kewra water before the preserve is cold. When cold, store the preparation in an airtight container, and serve when needed.

DRIED DATES PRESERVE

(CHHUHAARA MURABBA)

Serves	10 helpings or more
Preparation time	10 minutes plus soaking time
Cooking time	30 minutes

An odd preserve that is outstanding in its solitary grandeur! Keeping the stones inside the dates (although stones are not for eating) gives them something of a personality. Eating them will be a pleasure. A really cool dish in more ways than one!

Imperial (Metric)	American
1 lb (450g) dried dates	1 pound dried dates
1 teaspoon edible lime powder	1 teaspoon edible lime powder
Water as needed	Water as needed
1 lb (450g) raw cane sugar	2 cups raw sugar
2 teaspoons lemon juice	2 teaspoons lemon juice
2 teaspoons rose water	2 teaspoons rose water
Edible gold foil, to serve	Edible gold foil, to serve

1

Clean the dates and lightly, but carefully, prick them with a fork; make sure you do not break them open. Soak the dates in a mixture of lime powder and water for about 30 minutes. Then wash the dates in clean water, still keeping them whole.

2

Make a one-string syrup with the sugar and water as needed. Drop in the dates and keep cooking over a moderate heat for 10 to 15 minutes, until the dates are tender and the syrup thickens. Stir in the lemon juice, and remove the pan from the heat.

3

Before it cools off completely, add the rose water to the preparation. When cold, fill a clean and dry lidded, glass jar with the preserve.

4

Serve when needed; close the jar promptly after each use. Decorate each serving with a foil

BABACO PRESERVE

(Kamrakh Murabba)

Serves	*8 helpings*
Preparation time	*15 minutes plus soaking, drying, and melting time*
Cooking time	*25 minutes*

This delightful preserve, like others, is served cold in the morning and after meals. Unfortunately, babaco is not easily available everywhere, but a successful search will be well worth the reward!

Imperial (Metric)	*American*
8 medium, firm babacoes	8 medium, firm babacoes
1 teaspoon sea salt	1 teaspoon sea salt
1 tablespoon natural yogurt	1 tablespoon plain yogurt
Water as needed	Water as needed
1 lb (450g) raw cane sugar	2 cups raw sugar
1 tablespoon lemon juice	1 tablespoon lemon juice
Pinch of green cardamom powder	Dash of green cardamom powder
1 teaspoon rose water	1 teaspoon rose water
Edible silver foils, to serve	Edible silver foils, to serve

1

Wash the babacoes, and prick them all over with a fork. Make a mixture of salt, yogurt, and enough water, and soak the babacoes in it for 2 hours.

2

Wash the babacoes in several changes of clean water. Boil them in water about 5 minutes. Remove the pan from the heat, take out the babacoes, and let them dry.

3

Smear the babacoes with half the sugar and place them in a deep, lidded saucepan; cover the pan, and leave it overnight, or for at least 6 hours. The sugar will have melted into syrup.

4

Place the saucepan with babacoes over medium heat, and bring to a boil. Add the remaining sugar, and bring to another boil. Stir in the lemon juice, and remove the pan from the heat. Add the cardamom powder to the mixture. Before the preparation is completely cool, stir in the rose water.

5

When cold, store the preserve in a sterilized container of an adequate size; serve when needed. Decorate each serving with a foil.

LOQUAT PRESERVE

(Lukaat Murabba)

Serves   10 helpings or more

Preparation time   15 minutes plus soaking and melting times

Cooking time   30 minutes

Here is another exotic offering from India. Leave the stones inside the loquats when preserving — this lends a muscular texture to the dish. Serve cold as a dessert or at breakfast time. If gold foils prove hard to get, use silver ones instead.

Imperial (Metric)	*American*
2 lb (900g) ripe loquats	2 pounds ripe loquats
1 teaspoon sea salt	1 teaspoon sea salt
Water as needed	Water as needed
2 lb (900g) raw cane sugar	4 cups raw sugar
1 tablespoon lemon juice	1 tablespoon lemon juice
Large pinch of green cardamom powder	Large dash of green cardamom powder
Pinch of crushed saffron strands	Dash of crushed saffron strands
Edible gold foils, to serve	Edible gold foils, to serve

1

Wash the loquats gently; prick them all over, and then soak in a mixture of salt and water for about 30 minutes. Wash the loquats, carefully, in several changes of water.

2

Boil enough water in a saucepan to cover; drop in the loquats, and remove the pan from the heat. Cover the pan, and let it cool. Drain off the loquats, and gently rub off their outer skins.

3

In a separate saucepan, arrange the peeled loquats neatly, and cover with half of the sugar. Cover the pan, and leave overnight. By the morning the sugar will have melted into syrup and will also have entered the loquats.

4

Place the pan with loquats over moderate heat, add the remaining sugar, and cook until the loquats are tender (but do not let them break) and the syrup has assumed one-string consistency. Stir in the lemon juice, and remove the pan from the heat.

5

Add the cardamom powder and saffron to the preparation before it cools completely. When cold, store the preserve in a sterilized glass jar, and serve when needed. Decorate each serving with a foil.

AAMLA PRESERVE

(Aamla Murabba)

Serves	*20 helpings or more*
Preparation time	*15 minutes plus soaking time*
Cooking time	*45 minutes*

Aamla is a small, round citrus fruit with a slight bitterness in taste until it's cooked. It looks rather like a small, green, ping pong ball. It has a stiff outer skin and a big stone inside; when cut open its flesh displays several clear segments. The preserve made from aamla is cooling and has terrific rejuvenating potential. Varanasi aamla is the best variety.

Imperial (Metric)	*American*
2 lb (900g) firm, green aamlas	2 pounds firm, green aamlas
1 tablespoon edible lime powder	1 tablespoon edible lime powder
Water as needed	Water as needed
1 teaspoon alum powder	1 teaspoon alum powder
2 lb (900g) raw cane sugar	4 cups raw sugar
1 tablespoon lemon juice	1 tablespoon lemon juice
½ teaspoon green cardamom powder	½ teaspoon green cardamom powder
Silver foils, to serve	Silver foils, to serve

1

Soak the aamlas in a mixture of lime powder and water overnight. This will soften their outer skins. Wash the aamlas, and prick them thoroughly; soak them in a mixture of alum and water about four hours; this will remove the bitterness from them. Then wash in several changes of clean, cold water.

2

Place the aamlas and clean water in a deep saucepan, and bring to a couple of boils over moderate heat. Remove the aamlas, and put aside to dry.

3

Meanwhile, in a separate saucepan, make a one-string syrup with the sugar and water as needed. While the syrup is still on the stove, drop in the aamlas, and cook over a medium heat for another 10 minutes.

4

Stir in the lemon juice, and cook until the aamlas are tender and the syrup has thickened. Then remove the pan from the heat, add the cardamom powder, and let the mixture cool. When cold, store the preserve in an airtight container, and serve when required. Decorate each serving with a foil.

Index

175